To Val, Sophy and Giles

Acknowledgements

With my thanks to Lady Greenstock, Sir James Craig,
Sir Harold Walker, Maulvi Abdul Aziz, Mohammed Aslam
Aseem, Moukaram Atassi, Dr Saeed Mohammad Saeed
al-Barwani, Peter Bentley, Mohammad Yousef al-Budoor,
Dr Obaid Ali bin Butti, Christina Daftar, Mozna Daljani,
Michael Field, Philip Goddard, Julia Hoey, Anthony
Hunter-Choat, Shirley Kay, Philip Keating, Hugh Leach,
John Macfarlain, Dr Jehad al-Omari, Julian Paxton, Michael Tait,
Garth Wensley, Val Williams, Nikki Wilson, Chris Wilton, plus
a number of serving British and other diplomats, distinguished
Gulf Arabs and experienced Gulf expatriates of many
nationalities who prefer to remain unnamed. All provided many
helpful comments affecting this book for which I am enormously
grateful. My special thanks go to Ian Fairservice, Catherine
Demangeot, Anne Reynolds, Becky Taylor and Peter Burgess,
my publishers and editors at Motivate.

The illustrations were drawn by Kevin Cook, RIBA.

Caveat

This book, which is written for the use of Westerners going to live
in – or do business with the Arabs in – the Gulf, is naturally
written from a Western point of view. Where Western and Arab
attitudes and practices are compared, it should not be thought
either is necessarily taken to be preferable.

The book is always under review and all comments to update
it are particularly welcome.

JEREMY WILLIAMS
Bramdean, England
November 1998
e-mail: jjw@handshaikh.com
website: http://www.handshaikh.com

Don't they know it's Friday?

*Cross-cultural considerations
for business and life in the Gulf*

Jeremy Williams OBE

An imprint of Motivate Publishing

Published by **Motivate Publishing**

Dubai: PO Box 2331, Dubai, UAE
Tel: (+971 4) 282 4060, fax: (+971 4) 282 0428
e-mail: books@motivate.ae   www.booksarabia.com

Office 508, Building No 8, Dubai Media City, Dubai, UAE
Tel: (+971 4) 390 3550, fax: (+971 4) 390 4845

Abu Dhabi: PO Box 43072, Abu Dhabi, UAE
Tel: (+971 2) 677 2005, fax: (+971 2) 677 0124

London: Acre House, 11/15 William Road, London NW1 3ER
e-mail: motivateuk@motivate.ae

Directors: Obaid Humaid Al Tayer and Ian Fairservice

First published 1998 by Motivate Publishing
Reprinted 1999, 2001, 2003, 2004, 2005, 2006, 2007

© Jeremy Williams 1998

ISBN: 978 1 86063 074 3

British Library Cataloguing-in-Publication Data
Williams, Jeremy
Don't They Know It's Friday? Cross cultural considerations for business and life in the Arabian Gulf
1. Business etiquette – Arabian Peninsula
2. Business enterprises – Arabian Peninsula
3. Arabian Peninsula – social life and customs – 20th century
1. Title 382'.09536

Printed by Rashid Printers, Ajman, UAE.

NOTE ON MAPS: The maps in this book represent no authority on borders. They have been specifically designed for the sole purpose of illustrating the geographical extent of such entities as 'the Middle East', 'the Islamic World' and 'the GCC'. They have neither any purpose nor any relevance beyond this use.

Jeremy Williams

Jeremy Williams OBE was the Defence, Naval, Military and Air Attaché in the British Embassies of Abu Dhabi and Bahrain at the times of both the Iran/Iraq (the Tanker) War and the Gulf War. In an army career of 35 years he spent over 12 years in five Gulf locations: Sharjah, Dubai, Riyadh, Abu Dhabi and Bahrain. He was in contact with many government and commercial organisations throughout that time, both Western and Arab, particularly visiting or resident expatriates.

Jeremy Williams is a member of the Saudi-British Society, the Middle East Association, the Dubai Society, the Bahrain Society, the Royal Society for Asian Affairs and Middle East consultant to the Portsmouth University Language Centre.

His company, Handshaikh, is based near Winchester in England but he returns frequently to the Gulf to conduct business seminars and negotiation training which focus on the cross-cultural aspects of life and work in the countries of the Gulf. He has counselled over 200 companies. He and his wife, Val, have a daughter, Sophy and a son, Giles.

Contents

Foreword
by Sir James Craig GCMG

President of the Middle East Association,
33 Bury Street, St James, London, SW1Y 6AX

Some time ago a professor at the American University of Beirut wrote a book called 'Towards a Simplified Arabic' in which he recommended the removal of various irregularities in Arabic vocabulary and syntax so as to make the language easier to learn. On the day of publication he distributed complimentary copies to his colleagues in the Department of Arabic Language and Literature. One of them looked at the title and protested ruefully: "Professor, you're taking away our bread and butter".

I feel the same way about this book. Heavens above, it has taken me fifty years to learn something of the secrets of Arab society, Arab manners, Arab psychology. Is it all to be revealed in 124 pages by Mr Williams?

What I particularly like – rather grudgingly – about the book is that it gets the tone right. Some readers may think that it is too kind, too accommodating to the Arabs: the Westerner, for example, must be punctual at his appointments but suppress his wrath if the Arab is not. Yet the bottom line (if I may be allowed one contemporary vulgarism) is that when you go to another man's country you have to play by his rules.

Ah well then, doesn't it all boil down to the old proverb: 'when in Rome, do as the Romans do?' No, the book explains that it is more complex, more subtle than that. If Mr Smith wears Arab dress in Arabia he will be in trouble. Chapter 9 warns that if you use an Islamic greeting some Muslims may take offence. As well as simple rules, you need judgement, discretion, experience. Shakespeare can break the laws of English grammar but Mr Smith had better not – not, at least, till he has written a few plays and

sonnets and begun to feel at home with the subjunctive
and the conditional apodosis.

So take this book as a guide, the best I know. Trust it
without fear in your early days when you are new to the
region. Be very cautious about departing from its advice,
for it is full of information, common sense and good
manners, all reliable. But be prepared to adjust, modify
and learn, as you go along, from your Arab friends,
customers, agents, employees, bosses. The Arabs are not
one homogeneous entity. *Quot homines tot sententiae*, as
we used to say when the world was educated.

JAMES CRAIG

The Late Sir James Craig

One of Britain's most respected Arabists. Formerly lecturer
in Arabic at Durham University; principal instructor at the
Foreign Office, School of Arabic in the Lebanon; member
of the British Diplomatic Service in Dubai, Beirut, Jeddah
and Kuala Lumpur; Head of the Near East and North Africa
Department in the Foreign Office; British Ambassador to
Syria and Saudi Arabia; formerly visiting professor in Arabic
at Oxford; President of the Middle East Association and
President of the British Society for Middle East Studies.

1

The scope of this book

What does this book cover – and for whom?

The book focuses on the cross-cultural aspects of
Westerners' life and work with Arabs in the Gulf countries
of Kuwait, Saudi Arabia, Bahrain, Qatar, the UAE and
Oman. It does not cover, other than in general terms,
other Arab nations, nor is it a guide book on individual
Gulf countries. It will be of general use and interest to
many – but it is written with two main groups of
Westerners in mind.

Gulf-resident executives and frequent visitors to the Gulf

The first group of Westerners comprises business
executives who frequently visit, or who are resident in,
the Gulf. These include:

- Professionals, advisers and company executives –
  with or without their families.
- Business and government people who visit the Gulf.
- Men and women who need to know how to behave with
  Gulf Arabs in business generally, in negotiations and in
  personal etiquette.

Non Gulf-resident managers or infrequent visitors to the Gulf

The second group includes Western managers who do
not need to visit the Gulf frequently, if at all, but who
nevertheless have responsibilities for the selection,
tasking, evaluation and financing of company or
government staff employed in the Gulf. If company
interests are to be advanced realistically, such managers
should attempt to comprehend the nature of what their

colleagues in the Gulf frequently encounter.
These Westerners will include at least:

- Personnel Directors.
- Finance Directors.
- Human Resources staff, i.e. those who select, administer, fund or deploy personnel to the Gulf.
- General Managers who may, perhaps, have little or no knowledge of the everyday circumstances and tensions of life and work in the Gulf.
- Tourists to the Gulf – how to behave, what to wear and where.

General readers

This is also a book of interest to Western:

- Business and other executives who need an insight into the Gulf Arab mind.
- Professionals who have to arrange a visit by Gulf Arabs to a Western country.
- People who need an introduction to Islam, Islamic banking practice and the *Shariah* judicial system.
- Men and women who need information on various Arab groups such as the Arab League, OAPEC and the GCC.

Arab readers

In addition, the book caters to:

- Gulf Arabs who may wish to know how they are often regarded in the West.
- Gulf Arabs who are to attend education courses or training in the West.

Relationships between 'head office' and staff in the Gulf

Ideally, a common bond of understanding should exist between those in a Western 'head office' and those deployed on company or government business in the Gulf. All Western expatriates hope to be blessed that their 'head office' colleagues and managers have at least some introduction to or knowledge of the realities of Gulf life, and can therefore accept what may, and may not, be achievable for the company regardless of the performance of staff in-country. "I actually managed to speak to Shaikh Abdullah for five minutes about our project today!" is a major personal coup in Gulf terms, but for many in 'head office' such an encounter is hardly worth any form of congratulation or comment whatsoever. Gaining access[1] in the West, unlike the Gulf, is of no special remark.

The cost of failure

Unfortunately, many Western companies and individuals fail to face the realities of life and work in the Gulf. Many costly mistakes can be made, both financially and personally. Western companies sometimes believe that simply by dispatching highly qualified and intelligent staff to undertake duties in the Gulf all will be well. Foolish companies will presume that professional qualification is the overriding requirement and give no weight to the wider mental preparation (and selection) of such people and their spouses. Professional competence is the starting point for selection purposes; what is also needed, in the character of those under consideration for Gulf employment, especially in Kuwait and Saudi Arabia, are large measures of patience and resilience. This book addresses all these and many other such subjects and will be a helpful guide for all Westerners who have commercial or other activity in the Gulf.

---

1   See pages 4, 12, 44 and 58 on the important matter of 'access'.

2

General background

The importance of Islam

So important is Islam in the Middle East that some study
or acknowledgement of the subject is an essential element
of preparation for life in the Middle East. Chapter 18 gives
considerable additional information. Chapter 16 gives an
outline of *Shariah* law.

Islam is a binding force, not just throughout the region,
but beyond. Islam is more than a religion: it is a code of
behaviour and a way of life as well.

In those countries which enjoy neither democracy
nor the traditional Arab system of access to the ruler
(the *majlis* principle – where, traditionally, the ruler will
sit and take council among a gathered group of nationals),
extremist activity has often more to do with social
frustration and resentment at an inequitable distribution
of wealth than with religious belief. In such cases, Islam
may be the only respectable route for complaint.

The power and effect of Islam throughout the
Middle East and beyond may be difficult to comprehend for those who have not lived in the region for
any length of time.

Personality – the main factor?

This book looks mainly at the cross-cultural aspects of life
and business with companies and individuals in the Arab
Gulf Co-operation Council (AGCC) countries. It emphasises the behaviour, beliefs, habits, pressures and outlooks
of Gulf Arabs, some of which can overwhelm unprepared
business visitors, expatriates and families in the Gulf.
However, there will be many examples in the Gulf where

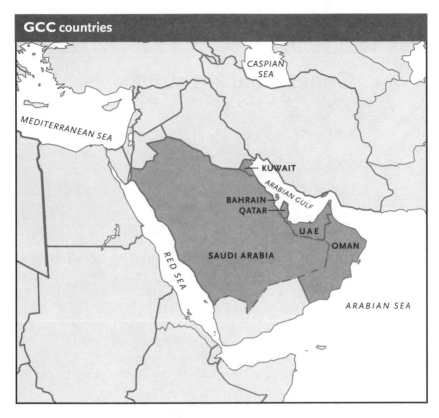

GCC countries

the personalities of the individual Gulf national and that of the expatriate will dominate their business and personal relationships – far more than any of the general cross-cultural considerations set out in this book.

Geography – grouping Arabs together

The term 'The Middle East' is very wide indeed. It is essential that those considering employment or activity in this region do not regard the geographic term as anything other than a very broad, historic and rather simplistic grouping of a number of quite different countries. Specific enquiries about the country or countries to be visited are essential. It is most important not to lump 'The Arabs' together or to treat 'The Middle East' as a single homogeneous entity. There are many variations, often within the

Muslim Countries of 'The Middle East'

countries themselves: in Saudi Arabia, for example, Western expatriate life in Jeddah is different from, and somewhat more relaxed than, that in Riyadh; whilst in the UAE marked differences of business style exist between Abu Dhabi and Dubai.

The countries

Traditionally, the term 'The Middle East' includes not only some of the countries of the Arab World – Bahrain, Egypt, Iraq, Jordan, Palestine, Kuwait, Lebanon, Oman, Qatar, Saudi Arabia, Syria, Turkey, United Arab Emirates (the UAE) and Yemen – but also Iran whose inhabitants are not Semitic but Indo-European and who speak Farsi/Persian, not Arabic.

Other neighbouring countries with Arab populations include Libya, the Sudan, Algeria, Tunisia and Morocco, the last three being known as the countries of the *Maghreb*[2]. The western border of the Middle East is usually taken to be the border between Egypt and Libya.

The Tiers

The Arab World as a whole can be divided into three general areas, namely: The Northern (or Levantine) region, North Africa, and The Arabian Peninsula and Gulf States. Divisions are also often made by commentators on the basis of rich/poor, stable/unstable or old/new. This book will focus primarily on living in and doing business in the Gulf States.

'Naming the Gulf'?

The coastline of the Gulf is shared between Iran (Persia) in the north and east, and a number of Arab states to the west and south. There is controversy concerning the geographic terms for 'The Gulf' and some cartographers will claim that there are two internationally recognised names. However, the prudent expatriate in any GCC country will not be drawn into discussion on the topic, and will simply refer to 'The Arabian Gulf' or just 'The Gulf', especially in the text or maps of business proposals or other documentation.

Arab groupings

The Appendix gives details of a number of Arab groupings including The Arab League, The Gulf Co-operation Council, and The Organisation of the Arab Petroleum Exporting Countries.

---

2   *Ghareb* = West; *Maghreb* = Westerning (of the sun).

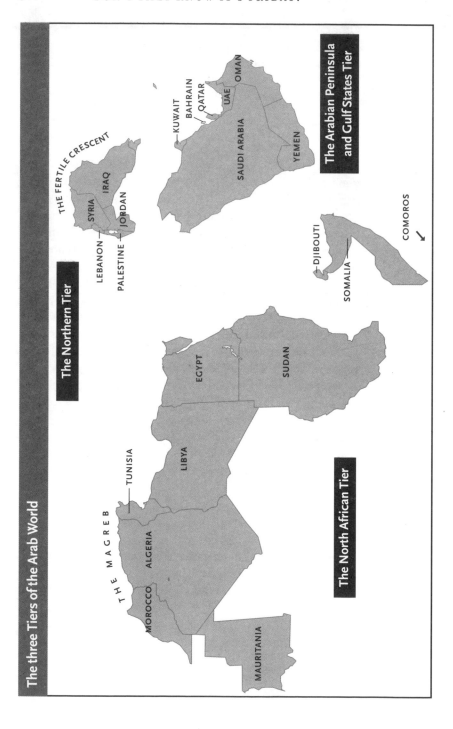

The three Tiers of the Arab World

The Northern Tier

THE FERTILE CRESCENT

SYRIA
IRAQ
JORDAN
LEBANON
PALESTINE

The Arabian Peninsula and Gulf States Tier

KUWAIT
BAHRAIN
QATAR
UAE
OMAN
SAUDI ARABIA
YEMEN

DJIBOUTI
SOMALIA
COMOROS

THE MAGREB

TUNISIA
LIBYA
EGYPT
SUDAN
ALGERIA
MOROCCO
MAURITANIA

The North African Tier

3

The expatriates

International presence

The Gulf draws international expatriates to its employment. The small number of nationals in all Gulf countries results in a dependence on foreign labour of one type or another. Such dependence is often resented by Arab nationals and there are occasional reduction exercises of expatriates in groups or individually, often peremptory, in an understandable attempt to stand nationals on their own feet. These initiatives have, in the past, been relaxed after a while, partly because there are insufficient nationals to undertake the full range of work needed by a modern nation. Few nationals are prepared to undertake non-managerial appointments, although this factor varies from country to country and depends on the population and per-capita income in each country.

Gulf nationals' employment

'Saudiisation', 'Omanisation' and 'Emiratisation' etc. (the names of the processes to place more nationals in jobs in their own countries) gathered momentum in the late 90s, more than ever before – far more so than in the 70s and 80s when similar 'nationalisation' was encouraged. Female nationals, particularly in the UAE and Oman, appeared to seize the opportunity to work, and are now increasingly seen in direct contact with the public in government offices and those of large companies, dressed demurely, heads always covered but without the veil. This is not so in Saudi Arabia – except that some Saudi women run businesses with a purely female clientele and that some Saudi women are owners or directors of ordinary businesses, but operate efficiently in the background.

Expatriates – national types

Expatriates come to work in the Middle East from all parts of the world. In some Gulf countries, the UAE for example, the ratio of expatriates to nationals can be as high as 80:20. Many Gulf manual labourers come from Yemen and very many from the subcontinent and the Philippines. Clerical and hotel staff in the Gulf come from, among other places, Egypt, Syria, Lebanon, India and Jordan. Specialist and managerial staff come from Australia, the subcontinent, Canada, France, Sweden, Germany, Denmark, Norway, Russia, the CIS countries, Ireland, the USA and the UK – in short, Gulf expatriates of a managerial or professional status come from most countries of the developed world.

Western expatriates – the two types

Western expatriates tend to fall into two main categories. The first comprises those who have specific proficiencies or skills, such as oilfield workers, telecommunications workers and manufacturing experts, while the second includes managers, trainers, advisers and professionals, who usually work in frequent direct contact with Arab nationals. Some of the latter group of expatriates are accompanied by their families.

Skilled Western worker status

This first group will often be unaccompanied, and will frequently undertake specialist duties as part of a corporate contract with the Arab country. Their employment therefore may not bring the workers concerned into regular contact with Arab nationals. Their wages and lifestyle (such as an allocation of accommodation and leisure facilities) usually form part of the company's overall arrangements in-country; these arrangements are likely to include an administrative department that will insulate employees from the full bureaucratic machinery of the host nation. This category of expatriate is likely to serve a two-year, usually non-renewable contract, often with the single-minded purpose of earning a specific cash sum, perhaps to pay off a debt, then to depart. Only limited adaptation to local ways may be needed, or attempted, by these expatriates, and therefore they may only become aware of the physical, as opposed to mental, difficulties of working in the Gulf.

Western managerial or professional status

However, the second category of expatriate has different problems. Salaries for these may be a matter for direct payment by Arab nationals, Arab companies or Arab governmental organisations and delays and interruptions in the regular payment of salaries by Arab organisations are rare but not unknown. They may have three-year contracts, often renewable on an annual basis thereafter. Others in this category may receive an allowance from their parent company and be expected to make their own arrangements for housing, cars, schooling, air tickets and so on. These expatriates are therefore subject to the full bureaucratic and cultural pressures of the Gulf.

Long-term Western expatriates

Some expatriates may have extended postings in the Gulf, perhaps as career moves within their companies. Others may repeatedly extend their personal contracts with Arab organisations and some may be abroad for 10–15 years, or even longer. Others have built up a business in partnership with Gulf nationals. A few expatriates 'retire' into their jobs: these are normally expatriates who have given 35–45 loyal years of service and who remain quietly in-country as advisers and friends, often remaining on their normal salary as a 'pension'. These latter expatriates can be fiercely loyal to their Arab organisations.

4

The selection process

Different

No one, especially Human Resources and Personnel staff, should be under any illusion about the very different life and working practices to be encountered by those who do business of any nature with countries and individuals of the Middle East, and this important fact must be borne in mind during the consideration of candidates for any Gulf activity. In general terms, the problem for Western visitors and expatriates sent abroad on company business is not so much one of living conditions (which are usually more than satisfactory) but the pace and style of work. The problems of apparent local indecision, the difficulty of gaining access to Arab decision-takers and the latter's reluctance to delegate even minor decisions, plus the lack of regard for time-keeping[3] all conspire to create stress for those accustomed to Western ways where an identifiable hierarchy, a clock and a diary are important and normal items.

Patience and resilience

Patience and resilience are probably the first two qualities needed, alongside professional competence, by those contemplating, or being considered for, employment in the Gulf. This is especially the case in Kuwait and Saudi Arabia but rather less so in Qatar, Abu Dhabi and Oman. In the opinion of most Westerners, Bahrain and Dubai are the 'easiest' business places – but only in terms of other locations in the Gulf.

---

3   See page 38.

A willingness to change and to adopt a more relaxed approach to local ways and methods is important for Western expatriates as Gulf Arabs can be almost impossibly frustrating in business negotiations, in timekeeping or when bargaining on price (see page 72). A sport, hobby or other out-of-office activity is therefore virtually essential.

Recruitment costs and stress generally

It is vital that the potential for stress in Westerners in, or in association with, the Gulf is acknowledged. Human Resources staff should take the greatest care before dispatching senior representatives and families to the Gulf since the cost of finding and preparing replacements, should those chosen fail, can be extremely high. The true all-up figure (which will include lost deposits, removal of children from school and so on) could be US$ 200,000 for senior staff. Time and care spent at the selection and briefing stages is rarely wasted. Candidates with short tempers should not be selected. It is essential that everyone receives an up-to-date and realistic briefing on the circumstances they and their accompanying families, if any, will face.

Women and the selection process

The restrictions that some (but not all) Middle East countries may impose on women should be specifically addressed in the selection process. This will often sit uneasily with normal company policy on equality of opportunity and with personal sensitivities, but, in extreme cases, failure to warn of the special pressures which Middle Eastern life can place upon expatriate women has been known to ruin careers or to break up marriages because the husband could not afford to give up his job and his wife could not handle the frustrations of living in the region.

Restrictions on women

In the Middle East women face restrictions on dress, and in Saudi Arabia in particular they also face restrictions over the men who may accompany them (in a car, at a restaurant, or on a journey, for example). Only men of the immediate family are acceptable, which poses problems for expatriate women who usually only have one close male relative available. Such a person is known in Arabic as a '*Mahram*' i.e. a woman's husband or any close blood relative whom she is forbidden to marry, i.e. father, brother, son etc. A woman may not appear in the company of a male whom she is, in law, permitted to marry, i.e. a male friend or colleague or, indeed, even her cousin. This restriction does not apply to a driver specifically employed as the 'family driver'.

Opportunities for the employment of women

In order to avoid being taken by surprise at treatment that in the West would be seen as discriminatory or unfair, women must be well briefed on the particular pressures which they may face. The prohibition on women as drivers in Saudi Arabia is the best known example, but women have also to accept that in certain Middle East countries their chances of employment are very limited. However, in other countries there are good opportunities for women which include managerial appointments, work with tourist firms, voluntary work, teaching English as a foreign language, medical appointments, secretarial appointments, full-time teaching, and a variety of temporary or seasonal jobs. In some Middle East countries normal semi-permanent job opportunities exist. Egypt, Bahrain, Oman and the UAE are probably the least restrictive, whilst (Saudi Arabia apart) Iran and Iraq currently offer the least attractive prospects for expatriate women. In Saudi Arabia, teaching and nursing are almost the only two legitimate employments open to expatriate women. In normally all cases, locally employed women will receive less favourable terms and pay than men.

Partners and risk of removal

The words 'wife' and 'husband' rather than 'partner' are deliberately used in this text since there is no chance whatsoever that 'partners' will be permitted to enter, for example, Saudi Arabia. In other places in the Gulf, where there is a far greater admission of foreign culture, and where entry is relatively easy for most foreign nationals, there is no significant day-to-day risk either on holiday or during business visits.

In rare cases, a malicious person, perhaps as a result of personal animosity or to damage a competitor's interests, could deliberately draw to the attention of the local authorities or influential Muslims the presence of an unmarried couple living openly together. As the civil authorities will not wish to become involved in matters of marital status, such events are not at all frequent and the matter should not be given undue weight. However, if the situation develops in such a way that the authorities can no longer ignore it, deportation will almost certainly follow (unless the couple have already departed voluntarily). Living together as partners is so alien to Islam that it cannot be ignored once formally and publicly known to the authorities.

Therefore those who are able to live together as partners in the Gulf for any time, and those who fund them, should recognise a small risk of disclosure and subsequent banishment with the attendant cost of establishing replacement staff. In company selection terms, the most practical approach is to accept that married or bachelor status is less complicated for resident Gulf appointments.

Ability to ignore

The matter of 'being able (or unable) to ignore' is important in many Gulf countries. A Westerner (or an Arab) who behaves in such a way that his actions 'cannot be ignored' places the authorities and others at risk in terms of public accusation of their own failure if they do not act themselves, even if they have no personal wish to take action.

Other relationships

Care will have to be given to the selection of those whose lifestyle includes same-sex (and therefore wholly un-Islamic) relationships: there is a risk of sudden deportation by local authorities (but probably only following public disclosure and accusation – see the previous paragraph). The consequential cost to the company of replacing such staff should be kept in mind at the selection stages even if Western practice and rules, in terms of discrimination, makes this extremely difficult, if not illegal.

5

Preparing to move to or visit the Gulf

Introduction

The comments that follow are not comprehensive since this is a book dealing mainly with cross-cultural matters, not the administration of visits[4] or moves to the Gulf. No attempt, therefore, is made below to cover every topic appropriate for every visit or family move to the Gulf. Nevertheless, what follows will be generally helpful, since it highlights a few, but important, issues. Current information must be sought – specific and relevant to the Gulf location and the Westerners involved – particularly when, for example, there is a mixed-nationality group of business visitors hoping to visit several countries as part of a Gulf 'tour'.

Travel

Travel by air to most countries of the Middle East (particularly the Gulf countries) is very easy, though it remains relatively expensive. There are many choices of carrier. Roads and internal air links are usually excellent. Rail, as a major transport system, does not exist in the majority of Middle East countries although the UAE is considering a Dubai/Abu Dhabi link[5]. Internal travel can be subject to bureaucratic difficulty and there can be restrictions on road movement.

---

4 See Chapter 17 on arranging a visit to the West for Gulf Arabs.
5 Khaleej Times (4 June 1998) reported that a German proposal was being considered.

Reconfirm flights

Take care to re-confirm the next leg of your flight having arrived in a Gulf country. Many carriers will cancel even a confirmed onward flight unless it is re-confirmed by you or your hotel at your request within, say, 24 hours of arrival. Be ready for considerable over-booking by some airlines of the Gulf, and have a plan to re-adjust your schedule should your confirmed (and re-confirmed) seat not be available to you at check-in. Stay calm. Be patient. Do not depend on the last flight for your departure – keep this as a back-up to an earlier flight. For peak times of travel, such as Christmas or other schoolchildren's holiday times, many expatriates will book seats months ahead of the dates of travel.

Visas

Visas are not always available for spouses and children since some contracts can demand bachelor status. The rule can sometimes be waived for highly qualified workers and professional expatriates, or where the employer has particular need of certain expatriate skills. Care should be taken over visas since EU arrangements have disturbed long-standing Middle East visa abolition agreements.

Passport validity

Besides enquiring into the Gulf visa situation, it is also wise to examine the dates of validity of all passports. If any passport is to expire within six months of the end of the planned visit or residence, it is probably best to apply for a replacement document. Also, any passport which contains an Israeli stamp should not be used, even in Saudi Arabia where, officially, there is no objection. In general, take care over visas, passport dates and Israeli stamps. Allow time for these matters to be resolved; do not leave things until the last moment[6].

---

6   Many sponsors (see page 78) will retain the passports of expatriate workers.

Driving licences

Most Western driving licences are acceptable for temporary hire car purposes in the Gulf. Most resident Western expatriates do not need to take a local driving test and are granted a local licence on presentation of their national licence. The regulations and the list of acceptable non-Gulf licences vary between Gulf countries and enquiry must be made. For example, Abu Dhabi has reminded expatriates of its Federal Traffic Law,[7] which lists 21 countries whose licences are acceptable – the list includes Japan and South Korea but does not include Australia, New Zealand and Singapore.

Photos

One of the items needed by visitors and new expatriates to the Gulf is a plentiful supply of passport-size photos. These are frequently required for all manner of administration and it is best to have many photos to hand, in order not to waste time arranging them in-country at short notice, thereby disturbing the visit or arrival programme. "I need two copies of your passport and five photos" is typical of the first requirement demanded by any official in the Gulf.

Culture shock

The profound differences between the way of life in the Gulf and that in the West can lead to severe culture shock. To some extent this can be alleviated by careful preparation and briefing before one leaves home. Reference libraries offer a wealth of books and magazines on the region and these should be consulted. Culture shock might not present problems to the seasoned traveller but can bring out serious symptoms in those who have not previously travelled much. It presents itself in various

7 Gulf News, 14 March 1998.

forms, ranging from simple homesickness to headaches and depression, as well as to more serious matters such as nervous disorders and breakdowns. Culture shock can be a prime cause of family disputes, divorce and, not surprisingly, eventual repatriation.

Confusion and disorientation

All too often, once the initial excitement of life in a new country wears off, and the strain of adapting to a new environment begins to tell, the expatriate comes to miss the familiar faces, places and objects that are taken for granted at home. There may be confusion over the differing values, cultures and customs of the new country; anxiety and even disgust can accompany some features of life abroad. If culture shock is taken into account well in advance, its worst symptoms can be reduced and even eliminated altogether. Essential pre-travel preparations should include learning as much as possible about one's new hosts: their way of life, foods, customs, traditions, and so on.

Take your leave

Some companies may offer their employees cash in lieu of leave or holidays. It is usually unwise to accept this arrangement since a build-up of stress is normal in the majority of Westerners working in the Gulf and the wise company will insist that leave, not cash, is taken. Take your leave; take a break.

Are you the problem?

Many Western expatriates take holidays in regions neighbouring the Gulf. This is normal, particularly for expatriates who have two-year contracts. However, for the longer-term expatriates, it is better to go home at least once in three years, preferably annually. Apart from recharging your batteries in your own culture, it is good to be reminded of the frustrations of living at home that, perhaps, had either been forgotten or been viewed through somewhat rose-coloured spectacles in the Gulf. Many expatriates, returning to the Gulf from 'mid-tour' leave at home, are more tolerant of Arab problems and methods, having been reminded that 'home' also has its problems.

Many expatriates will notice that a hurdle that had existed before leave, and had seemed insurmountable, has somehow evaporated during the leave period; in many cases it was the expatriate who was the problem, and who was simply in need of leave. For those with three-year (or longer) contracts, the most productive period in the Gulf is often the six months following a good period of leave away from the Gulf.

6

Behavioural differences

The West v. the Gulf

Most visitors and expatriates can be guided by the basic rule that if behaviour is unacceptable or offensive in the West generally, then it will be unacceptable in the Middle East as well. Although judicial processes and punishments differ, public attitudes are very similar towards drugs, drinking and driving, and, in particular, theft. Rude or aggressive behaviour and the wearing of very skimpy clothing in public places are also widely deprecated. Regional differences in attitude are also important and specific advice should be taken. For example, tight and short clothing in Saudi Arabia, worn by either sex, is unacceptable and can result in arrest (particularly for women), whereas in Oman and the UAE such clothing would be regarded by the nationals as merely an inept lack of understanding of local customs and sensibilities.

Stupidity...

Selling alcohol to Muslims and criticising Islam are two activities in the Middle East which are either illegal or singularly stupid. Less obviously, add for the Middle East:

- Regarding the terms 'The Arabs' and 'The Middle East' as useful expressions, and not enquiring into the very different characteristics and circumstances found in Arab nationals and their nations. 'Lumping Arabs together' is quite wrong (see page 5).
- Not taking the greatest possible care in the selection of a company sponsor (see page 78).

- Wearing revealing clothing (especially for women off-the-shoulder or short dresses, and for men shorts and cut-away vests) in public places such as markets (see page 24).
- Signing any document in Arabic which is not understood.
- Kissing a member of the opposite sex in public (see page 35).
- Writing a cheque against which there are no funds. Bouncing a cheque can be a criminal offence in the Gulf, not just a commercial matter.
- As a non-Muslim woman not thinking long and hard about children when considering marriage to a Muslim. (This comment holds good for any prospective cross-religion marriage, not just one involving a Muslim.) A Muslim husband will almost certainly regard his children to be Muslim at the point of birth. He is likely to consider them to be a non-negotiable component of his wider family and therefore, should the marriage fail, his attitude after the divorce, and that of his family will, in most cases, be absolute towards his assumption of the custody of the children.
- Having a dog in a car in which Arabs are passengers, or having a dog in the same room if entertaining or conducting business with Arabs. Almost all Arabs

Abdullah, I hope you don't mind a few dog hairs.

regard dogs as unclean and can be particularly uncomfortable in their presence. An exception may be the saluki, a desert hunting dog.

Clothing

As tourism increases in certain parts of the Gulf, such as Dubai, short or inappropriate clothing is increasingly seen on Westerners. The Russians are probably in the lead in this respect although Britons and Germans, especially those on package tours, are not far behind. 'Inappropriate' in this context means the wrong clothing (such as tight T-shirts, bathing costumes, bikinis, short dresses, off-the-shoulder dresses with shoulders and arms fully revealed, and cut-away vests and shorts) worn in public places such as shopping areas and supermarkets. Where tourism exists in the Gulf, holidaymakers should wear holiday clothing in holiday places, e.g. within the confines of hotel areas, pools or the beach, not in the *souq* (market) or other

public places in full Muslim view. Whilst there can, perhaps, be some margin of forgiveness for transient visitors (such as tourists) who fail the dress code, Westerners who are resident in the Gulf cannot be excused for such behaviour since it indicates a consistently rude, even arrogant, disregard for local norms.

Clothing in Saudi Arabia

In Saudi Arabia additional covering for women, i.e. ankle-length dresses (not clinging) and with arms covered to below the elbow, would be appropriate for those few women able to obtain visas to enter the country on business in company with male colleagues. Specific advice should be sought from your embassy in Riyadh as there may well be objections to too strict an adherence to full Islamic dress by expatriate women. For example, the wearing of the veil is highly unlikely to have the support of a Western Ambassador, as this could set a precedent for Western and other nationals and invite further Islamic dress restrictions. A balance needs to be drawn between showing proper respect for the wishes and practice of the host nation, and the normal behaviour of the Western visitor.

Visiting managers take heed

Managers who visit their Gulf-resident staff should take heed if their staff are casual in their choice of clothing in public: if staff cannot respond even to this most simple of local sensitivities, what other more sophisticated aspects of local affairs are they failing to grasp on behalf of the company? Respect local traditions; do not place the host nation at risk of condemnation from neighbouring Gulf countries or influential Islamic individuals; understand that the Gulf is a small village in terms of its peoples' ability and wish to observe and maintain close contact with one another. If one part of the Gulf grants too much licence in Westernised behaviour it will quickly be known and commented on elsewhere in the Gulf (and in the wider Arab and Islamic worlds). Foreigners who dress scantily in public in the Gulf are therefore particularly tactless, and obviously so.

Sense of humour

The Arab sense of humour is well developed and can provide a useful bridge to establish relationships.

Patience and the benefit of study

Most Arabs are hospitable and patient at the personal level. Many will excuse and forgive, albeit often in sorrow and disbelief, the ineptitude of a foreigner's behaviour in their countries, even if it is not comprehended. Arabs usually assume that Western visitors and new residents will be ignorant of Islam and the Arab way of life. It follows, therefore, that when the exception is discovered, i.e. a Westerner or any foreigner who has taken the trouble to learn a little Arabic and Arab customs, then that person is regarded as somewhat special – one deserving additional attention and welcome.

Awareness of the West

Many Arabs, Gulf Arabs in particular, are well travelled internationally and have a far greater understanding and tolerance of Western ways and norms than Westerners have of Arab life and business. Many own extensive properties in the West and may have received American and/or British education. Some travel frequently and are international people of considerable sophistication, confidence, intellect and ability, capable of holding their own in perfect English in international conferences and gatherings. The third and fourth generation of Arabs whose great-grandparents were desert bedouin or Gulf fishermen or pearl-divers are now emerging to reach important positions of power. They are unlikely to take offence at simple mistakes by a person new to Arab social behaviour and equally unlikely to place a foreigner in a situation which causes serious embarrassment, as this would not be hospitable and being inhospitable is wholly unacceptable behaviour to an Arab.

Condescension

It is most unwise to initiate a conversation that emphasises foreign influence[8] in Gulf external policy and defence matters: this may be thought condescending. Likewise, those who were once teachers, advisers or instructors of Arabs, either in the Gulf itself or in training establishments, should not expect special favours. These favours may or may not come, but would not be helped in any way by the adoption of superior airs. "Men in suits with noses in the air" was one Arab's plain summary of his perception of Western (particularly British) activity in the Gulf. Whether this is a wholly fair description of all Westerners throughout the Gulf could be challenged, but there is no doubt that certain styles of behaviour and mannerism can be taken very badly indeed.

One senior Western visitor, calling on a member of a Gulf ruling family on a matter affecting aviation, spoke of the local airport as being "about the same size as one of our small provincial airports" when the airport concerned is bigger than the second largest in the visitor's country. The remark was patiently and graciously received but it managed to be both condescending and wrong in equal measure.

Dangers of paternalistic attitudes

The Gulf Arab will understandably resent any trace of colonialism or patronage. "We hope to co-operate with you in making this project a success..." or: "As your own experts will have told you, this system has been adapted specifically to meet your needs..." is a much more positive approach than "We have come here today to instruct you in..." or: "Our government policy prevents us from releasing this

---

8 In the past the UK; the US now.

modification, so we are not able to agree to your request…" (Many Arabs will understand perfectly well that certain classified features may not be cleared for export to their country.)

Driving habits

The excellent roads of the Gulf countries lend themselves to fast driving and therefore to good communications between population centres. Modern, expensive, fast, air-conditioned cars are the norm. Most Gulf Arabs learn to drive at an early age and the majority develop good physical skills at the controls although the concept

Traffic accidents

If involved in an accident, stop. Be patient. Be calm. Do not move the vehicle unless the situation (such as the blockage of a bridge at rush-hour when damage to vehicles involved is minimal) clearly demands that it should be moved. If a resident, report to your sponsor by telephone at once if possible, and certainly shortly after the event if not. Wait for the police to arrive even if the incident is minor and even if no one has been hurt, because in many Gulf countries it is not permitted to repair any vehicle damage, however small, without a police report. Expect the police to rule on site who was to blame for the accident and to report accordingly. (Note: many constables are expatriates from non-Gulf Arab countries, such as the Sudan, but their superiors, who usually have military ranks, are almost invariably Gulf nationals.) Expect the judicial process to side with the police report and be prepared for severe penalties if you have been drinking, regardless of the facts or fairness of the particular incident and even, for example, if you have been hit from the rear. Be polite to the other party, especially if that person is a national, since he may be prepared to speak favourably to the police if you are calm and reasonable in demeanour, but he will certainly not be helpful if you are rude and aggressive. A crowd of onlookers will almost certainly quickly form and other traffic will generally slow down to observe the scene. Be calm and behave quietly. This is not your country, and extravagant behaviour such as shouting and pushing will only work against your interests; your performance will merely provide free amusement for the onlookers, including the police, who will not be well disposed towards those who display what they consider (and indeed what would be) ugly foreign behaviour.

Pedestrians

Arab ladies, fully covered, will sometimes cross a road in a city or town with confidence, assuming that traffic will stop or slow to allow their passing, which it does. The expatriate driver, normally accustomed to pedestrians at marked crossings only, should take care. However, expatriates on foot waiting at pedestrian crossings should not assume that traffic will stop and should therefore cross only with caution.

of lane discipline still has some room for development. The essential quality for all drivers in the Gulf is to drive defensively and with great caution at junctions and round-abouts (especially) and not to become angry. 'Patience', an essential quality needed in all who live and work in the Gulf, is never more in demand than on the roads.

Acceptance of gifts

The natural inclination of Gulf Arabs is to be welcoming, hospitable and generous to guests and strangers. This trait can manifest itself in the giving of gifts, sometimes on a lavish scale. Many Westerners are cautious when offered gifts by business associates and many prefer to decline them. But a balance must be drawn between the offence which might be given to the host if a gift is clumsily refused against the risk of indebtedness which may accrue to the host by the acceptance of a gift. Caution is needed in most cases.

Photography

Most people do not enjoy strangers deliberately and publicly taking their photographs without their permission and this is as true in the Gulf as anywhere else. There are Islamic dimensions to be considered as well: Islam condemns all forms of 'graven image' and personal aggrandisement and some Muslims will claim that this restriction embraces the photography of humans. Where an important Gulf figure is clearly and publicly carrying out an official or similar duty, such as prize-giving, there are no objections to photography; it may even be expected and welcome. But openly to take pictures of Arab women in the market, for example, is intrusive and lacks sensitivity and should be avoided. Photography near military installations could lead to arrest in almost all Gulf countries.

"We just wanted to make you happy"

There is a reluctance in most Gulf Arabs [9] to be the bearers of bad news. This trait can cause great stress to Westerners accustomed to dealing with, and adjusting to, the realities – good or bad – of any situation as it unfolds. For many Gulf Arabs it is thought better to cloak the harsh truth until such time as it reveals itself, or to let someone else make it known. Many Arabs will concur that it is kinder to let the person concerned gently deduce himself that a problem exists rather than be told about it bluntly.

One young Arab was told that his grandfather was sick. Over the next day or so he was told that his grandfather was becoming progressively more ill, when in fact his grandfather had already died some days before. It was thought kinder to let the boy become prepared for bad news over a period of time rather than simply to present him with the stark fact of his grandfather's death without warning.

One Westerner applied for a business visa to visit Oman. There was an administrative problem. The Westerner was assured from Oman throughout three days that there was "No problem, your visa will be issued in five to ten minutes and will be given to your airline in Muscat so that you can collect it when you arrive." For three days he was refused boarding on six aircraft to Muscat from Dubai because the visa had not been issued. The administrative problem was never explained to the Westerner.

---

9   And expatriates from the subcontinent.

Face

The matter of 'face' and 'saving face' has some importance when dealing with Gulf Arabs. The concept of 'face' may not be as well developed or acute in the Gulf as may be the case in the Far East, or in countries of Latin temperament, but the Western expatriate should be particularly cautious when dealing with a situation which might suggest a fault by, or limitation in, a Gulf Arab, especially if the matter is brought into public knowledge, such as at an office meeting. Saying "I made a mistake" or "I was wrong; it was my fault" can be particularly difficult for many people and such reluctance is as true in the Gulf as anywhere else in the world. Quick (but usually cold and silent) offence can be taken, often leading to dismissal and the departure of the expatriate, possibly even that very day. Other reaction may be more subtle and can include the deliberate, widespread but discreet blocking of the business and other interests of the Westerner, including those of the company he represents in the Gulf. It is best never to provoke a deliberate and open confrontation with a Gulf Arab regardless of the truth or other factors in the case. 'Reputation' is a component of Gulf Arab sensitivity towards the loss of 'face'. See page 77 concerning the expectation (and preference) of strong leadership by Gulf Arabs, and page 81 concerning 'reputation' in general.

Take the blame

The experience of Westerners with Gulf Arabs is that the overwhelming majority are courteous, patient and good colleagues and employers. But the sensible Westerner will not 'confront' anyone in the Gulf and will try to lead a quiet and moderate business life, with 'patience' being the watchword in all dealings.

In the matter of 'face', as shown above, most people know at once when they have made a mistake. Most, including Gulf Arabs, will be far better disposed towards others who clearly know the details but who do their best to handle everything in a way that does not involve the loss of 'face' by anyone. In this respect it may be necessary for the Westerner to shoulder some or all of the blame, even if this is personally or professionally particularly hard: "I'm sorry. I haven't explained the situation clearly enough. It's my fault there is a misunderstanding." The best way to indicate a problem to a Gulf Arab is to do so in a private place, calmly and gently – and when the person concerned is in the mood to receive unfavourable news. If the subject is not vital, i.e. not a matter of safety or serious risk, it may often be simpler not to raise it at all.

7

Personal behaviour, body language

Shaking hands with men and women

The normal – perhaps essential – male behaviour on meeting a Gulf Arab under any circumstances is to stand up if seated and to shake hands, saying "*As-Salaam Alaykum*" (see page 50). But for a man to shake the hand of a Gulf Arab woman (and vice versa) is not normal and there appears to be no simple rule of etiquette to follow. If the Arab woman is Westernised and the meeting is in international circumstances, such as at a prominent hotel in the Gulf, or in the West itself, she might extend her hand to be shaken by a Western or Arab male acquaintance, since she will know that this activity is normal Western behaviour. But in the Gulf (and absolutely in Saudi Arabia) it is unlikely that a woman will offer her hand to be shaken.

Modest dress

Expatriates in Saudi Arabia often refer to 'Religious Police' but the police are usually only in attendance to the *mutawwa* (Guardians of Morality) who will approach and remonstrate with those who are not dressed modestly. There is an additional 'husband factor' which strongly reinforces the need for females to dress moderately and not to cause local offence. Since an expatriate female must be accompanied by her husband in public (there is usually no other *mahram* – see page 14 – available except her husband) and few husbands will stand idly by if their wives are addressed harshly, a confrontation may occur, perhaps involving shouting and other unpleasant activity – even violence. It is therefore much better for everyone if the requirement for modest dress in Saudi Arabia is respected.

The sensible Western male will, therefore, if introduced to mixed-sex Gulf Arab company (which is quite rare), hold back from shaking the hands of women and will not initiate the act. He should watch and mimic the behaviour of Gulf males in the group. Likewise, the female Westerner should not extend her hand to be shaken by a Gulf male unless she is content that no embarrassment will ensue: it is possible that a fervent Muslim will refuse her hand, almost certainly politely apologising for being unable to do so. A good rule is: same sex – definitely shake hands, even embrace; different sex – do not even shake hands, hold back.

Holding hands

Many male Arabs will hold hands with one another without the act indicating anything other than simple, uncomplicated friendship or fondness for another member of the family, or good acquaintance. Male Arabs can often be seen walking together, gently holding hands without embarrassment. Arab women rarely, probably never, hold hands with other women in public, although the linking of arms is not unknown. It is not normal for an Arab to hold hands in public with a member of the opposite sex.

Kissing

Most Arabs of the same family, or of close acquaintance, will greet one another with a kiss to one or both cheeks. The forehead, nose and parts of the *shemagh* (headdress) can be involved in this ritual. The degree and method of the embrace vary and can signal different degrees of friendship and relationship, such as that between father and son, or that between ruler and citizen.

It is very rare indeed for men and women to embrace in public in the Middle East; visitors and expatriates should remember and respect this fact. In certain Gulf countries the police might arrest the couple, particularly if a fervent Muslim complains to the police in such a way that the couple's activity cannot be ignored. Most Gulf policemen would probably wish to avoid confronting or arresting a Western couple for actions which were merely insensitive, but if their attention is drawn openly to such non-Islamic behaviour, they have little personal or professional option but to proceed, as good Muslims, with an arrest. The solution for men and women is not to kiss one another in public in the Middle East. In the more liberal Gulf countries, where arrest is unlikely, most Arabs will wearily regard such behaviour as yet another example of Western ill-preparedness for the norms of personal conduct in the Gulf.

Exposed flesh

Many Arabs are embarrassed by the display of flesh, e.g. shorts worn by males in public, and find the tolerance of this habit by Westerners as particularly strange. Where Western newspapers are sold in the Middle East pictures showing the shoulders and other parts of the body may be blacked out by the local distributor as a condition of sale of the newspaper. Where there is too much flesh for this censorship to be possible, the whole print-run may be withdrawn; that edition of the publication will not appear. In Saudi Arabia (and other parts of the Gulf as well) the female shoulders etc. on soap powder boxes and similar

packaging are also blacked out. The message for
expatriates is clear throughout the Middle East: dress
modestly or (in some countries) risk the spraying of
ankles and shoulders from spray-paint cans wielded by
fervent Muslims who are accompanied by the police.

The soles of feet

Many Westerners are convinced that the display of the
soles of feet always causes offence to all Arabs. This is one
of two topics (the other being the sheep's eye; see page 87.)
which have become so engrained in the West's perception
of the Arab way of life that it is difficult to change or
remove them. Since walking barefoot across the desert
makes the feet dirty (and water for washing may be in
short supply), it is probable that in the past it made
particularly good sense not to display one's feet in
company; it is still considered polite not to do so.
In Western terms, placing the feet aggressively on
a table in full view of others, soles showing or not, is an
unpleasant gesture and offensive by any standards; the
same disagreeable effect will be experienced by Arabs.

Beckoning with the fingers

In many regions of the Middle East, to ask someone to
approach you by beckoning with the upright forefinger is
distinctly rude, as is the defiant gesture of disapproval
indicated by the raising of a digit finger from a clasped fist
on an extended arm. The latter gesture is known to be, and
usually intended to be, rude in any society. But the former
gesture involving an upright forefinger may be made quite
unconsciously by a Westerner in an Arab country. Care
is therefore needed not to give offence. The equivalent
and acceptable gesture is either (1) to draw, from the
horizontal, the whole extended arm pointing at the
other person down to your side, or (2) to turn your palm
over and pull all the fingers quickly a few times into an
upside-down fist, normally with the outstretched arm
pointing in the direction of the other person.

Right   *Wrong*

Crossed legs

There is a lesser gesture, involving crossed legs, often
made quite unconsciously by a Westerner. This is when
the foot on the upper crossed leg is pointed directly and
frequently in the direction of an Arab. The foot, when
'bounced on the knee' in the general direction of an
Arab, can cause discomfort, perhaps even distaste, since
it may symbolise, in body language terms, an accusing or
threatening weapon. The solution is not to cross the legs
when in company with Arabs or, if this is not convenient,
then to take care where the foot is pointed.

8

Time and timing

Time-keeping – the biggest frustration?

Probably all Westerners in the Gulf will quickly agree that
the frequent inability of their Gulf colleagues to keep to
time is the most significant of all the cross-cultural aspects
affecting their work in the Gulf. But many Gulf Arabs will
comment that they are always available at any time and
that access to them is simple. They may claim that it is
only the unavoidable and unforeseen accident of other
duties – such as those involving the family or friends[10] –
or unexpected duties placed necessarily on them by
members of ruling families that draw them away from
agreed meetings with Westerners.

*Abdullah, could we move next month's
meeting from 11.20 to 11.40?*

---

10   See page 65 for further comment on the placement of family, friends,
     Muslims and strangers in Gulf life.

Westerners normally have no concept of the absolute duty that Gulf Arabs have towards family situations which are, in general, far greater than those undertaken, or expected, in Western society. "My brother telephoned and asked to see me, so I had to go to him; I am sorry I had to miss our meeting" is typical of the remark a Gulf Arab might make to a Westerner after a failed meeting i.e. genuinely believing that the explanation – because it involved a family member – would be understood, and failing to comprehend that for the Westerner such a reason would not be good enough. The Westerner would have been far less bothered if a phone call rearranging the meeting had been received, but the experience of almost all Westerners is that most Gulf Arabs do not reschedule meetings beforehand – they simply fail to appear when expected. 'Time' is therefore a major area of culture clash.

The younger Gulf Arab

Many of the younger Gulf Arabs are fully aware of the West's distaste for bad time-keeping. A minority is entirely capable of organising their life and business along Western lines. The younger Gulf business person would probably reject as outdated and simplistic the excuse mentioned above. Many Gulf Arabs, young or old, do their genuine best to keep to time when in company with Westerners, even though they may never comprehend what they probably regard as a cold Western fascination with the 'minor' matter of time.

Centralism and its power

In the centralised societies of the Gulf countries, power of decision rests with a number of personalities from significant or ruling families. All individuals, especially those of any consequence, are permanently on call to attend to the wishes and instructions of such families. The effect is that any Gulf Arab can find himself suddenly accompanying a member of the ruling family or other important Gulf personality on, for example, a week's

visit to a foreign country with only a few hours' notice –
and sometimes with no notice whatsoever. This means
that the individual's way of life, personal as well as
professional, must be totally set aside – the 'diary' is
therefore almost irrelevant, all the time.

Westerners, who may not be able to comprehend that
such a way of life could possibly exist for any time, can be
assured that it indeed endures throughout all the Gulf
countries. It is difficult for most senior Gulf Arabs to
make, or keep, any appointment with confidence, even
if they indicate full prior agreement. When an important
meeting is being proposed, most Gulf Arabs genuinely
expect, and probably want, to attend it. Only other,
unforeseeable, and usually unavoidable, factors will
prevent their attendance.

Gulf Arabs mean no offence when meetings fail to take
place. Many may find no special need to inform visitors
ahead of time in their hotels, for example, that a meeting
must be cancelled. Many are concerned at, but are
perhaps surprised by, the bother that failed meetings
cause to Westerners since, in their own society, there is
no special need deliberately to 'inform' other parties of
changing situations; the excellent grapevine of local
gossip and knowledge – to which the mobile phone has
added greatly – alerts everyone of importance to the new
arrangements. The best expatriates will seek to make
themselves party to such networks and will therefore
never need to be surprised to hear the words on arrival
for a meeting: "Oh, didn't you know? – he's in Morocco;
he went last night with his father."

Coping with a VIP visit to the Gulf

One very senior and charming Gulf Arab, asked by a
Western official if he would receive an important
Western dignitary in a week's time, said: " I know him
well and I will of course be delighted to receive him –
if I am in the country." Such a remark gave no confidence
whatsoever in terms of writing the important visitor's
programme, but it was an entirely accurate and reasonable

Gulf reply. The experienced Gulf expatriate executive should regard the problems of any senior Gulf visit as being in two parts: (1) head office's perception and (2) the realities of managing the visit on-site, on the day. The first task is to deal with (1). This is achieved by submitting a programme some weeks or months ahead, and not indicating that it is almost certainly inaccurate, in whole or in part, as indeed will be the case. If doubt is indicated, there will be no peace from 'head office', from where the demands for a 'proper' i.e. 'confirmed' programme will be unceasing – and increasingly strident as the VIP's departure date for the Gulf approaches.

The expatriate, having dealt with 'head office' as described, should now keep generally in touch with the appropriate Gulf personalities and their secretaries as the visit date approaches. Contact should be made a week before, two days before, one day before and perhaps on the very morning of the day itself. The frequency of such precautionary and repeated contact will vary between organisations and personalities, and the expatriate must judge whether such continual contact is needed, or whether it might be taken amiss. If in doubt, err on the side of repeated contact, but in a relaxed and pleasant manner.

An important Arab, the focus of one particular Western VIP's visit, when told that the VIP had arrived, said: "Oh, is he here, now, today? – Bring him to me now, I will give him lunch". This was a classic example of generous Arab hospitality, made on the spur of the moment, and perfectly

Cross-cultural tensions

These paragraphs are offered somewhat 'tongue-in-cheek' but the comments will nevertheless illustrate the kind of cross-cultural tensions of working for a Western organisation in the Gulf as a Western expatriate. Some expatriates will claim that they have no problems with their Arab colleagues, only with their 'head office'. See page 49 concerning the need for realistic relationships between 'head office' and its Gulf-resident staff

sincerely, but it completely wrecked the arrangements
already in place for the VIP to address an important
Western lunch elsewhere to which many from the
expatriate community had been invited.

The VIP therefore had two lunches and joined the
second quite late which caused a great Western fluttering,
especially in the minds and behaviour of the newer
expatriates and their spouses who had other matters to
address that afternoon. The fact that they heard the VIP's
speech at the end of the lunch, rather than at its start, was
of unnecessary (but very real) concern to many present,
much bothered that the visit programme was not running
to plan, and to time.

In the course of that day the VIP met everyone whom
he had expected to meet – but not in the order shown in
his programme (even the updated version provided for
him on arrival in-country). This gave his accompanying
staff much to worry about, disturbed by, and wholly out
of their depth with, the sudden and frequent changes of
programme and timing. In short, these visitors and the
VIP himself had experienced, personally and perhaps for
the first time, the normal realities of business and official
life in the Gulf.

For the VIP it did not matter (or at any rate it ought not
to have mattered) at all 'how', 'where' or 'when' he met
those whom he needed to meet. What mattered to him,
and likewise to his Arab hosts, was that he achieved the
purpose of his visit by having conversations with people
who mattered – and in this case he had an added bonus,
at the unexpected lunch, because he met many additional
and influential Arabs who were not 'in the programme,'
and who themselves, doubtless, had had no idea when
they awakened that day that they would be lunching with
a foreign VIP. They would have received a call to attend
the lunch – probably with no warning whatsoever –
but from a personality who could not be ignored.
'Visit programmes' are therefore a source of rich cross-
cultural stress and nail-biting for Westerners. Things
usually work out satisfactorily, or even better than
expected, on the day of the visit itself.

Islam's influence on time-keeping

As well as Islamic undercurrents at play in all matters of 'time' and 'the future' there is the influence of former desert or seafaring life on many Gulf families. For the Muslim, and others, God alone controls the future and therefore any attempt to lay down what shall happen in the future, such as agreeing a date or time, is presumptuous and, for the very religious, borders on the blasphemous. In historical terms, life in the desert or at sea was without watches and diaries and 'time' was dictated by the sun and the call to prayer [11]. There was no need for, or inclination towards, more precise arrangements. "Speak to me after the dawn prayer tomorrow" was a sufficient remark in terms of planning.

The more cynical Westerner will observe that when a Gulf Arab wishes to be on time, then perfect time-keeping is the norm. Gulf Arabs are always 'sensible' about their interests, as are most people, anywhere.

It's not 'time' that matters – it's 'timing'

Most Gulf Arabs are aware that Westerners make great efforts to keep to time. Arabs know that keeping to time, and keeping to an agenda, are important in the West. They recognise that lateness is regarded as impolite, inefficient and usually disrespectful. Many Arabs find such precise habits to be strange, querying why it is appropriate, for example, to raise a subject dogmatically with an influential person at a specific time and place (such as at an office meeting as an agenda item) when the person concerned appears not to be in the right mood to be receptive or helpful.

When the moment is right

Most Arabs will delay matters until the mood, moment and place are all conducive to the raising of the topic, since the

---

11   See Chapter 18, page 113.

response is likely to be more favourable under such circumstances. Arabs find it odd that Westerners will plough ahead with unpopular subjects simply because the clock and agenda indicate that they should. Arabs regard both these latter items as servants, not masters. The effect, in Western terms, is that gross delay can ensue until 'the right moment' arrives.

Wait, wait, wait, – hurry, hurry, hurry

Westerners are usually hopelessly unaware of the personal relationships and general local undercurrents which dominate Arab decision-taking in the Gulf. They are therefore well advised to be patient. But they should always be ready to act very quickly once an Arab decision to proceed has been taken. This can occur quite without warning and usually follows the gaining of access to an important, and normally very busy, decision-taker. As a rough guide, 95% of time spent in Gulf business activity

will be spent waiting, followed by a 5% period of intense
work against impossible deadlines.

"No one came to our presentation – they all went to the airport instead!"

Western government officials and business people are
often invited (see box) to present a topic of interest to Gulf
Arab audiences. Much preparatory work and rehearsal is
done in the West, often at very short notice, with care and
concern, and with many pressing matters set aside in
order to come to the Gulf. Special funding and other
arrangements, official as well as personal, will be made.
These visitors will therefore be more than surprised –
angered – to find out on the day in question, even on the
morning itself, perhaps just as the presentation is due to
start, that the relevant audience has failed to appear, or
that some minor and often irrelevant official has been told
to receive the briefing at short, or no, notice. Such
rudeness, in Western eyes, is inexcusable. For military or
government visitors, accustomed to a structured way of
life, the conduct of the audience is completely
unbelievable.

What may not be appreciated by the visitors is that the
audience, or the senior members of it, may have been
advised at impossibly short notice that, for example, an
important dignitary is to arrive or depart at the main
airport in half an hour. It is the customary (and usually
unavoidable) practice for those who are important in the
community (or who regard themselves as important) to
gather at the airport in order to greet or to bid farewell to

Saying 'no'

Sometimes Westerners will suggest to Gulf Arabs that a
presentation on a particular topic would be helpful. They can
misread the Arab reaction: to be polite, many Arabs will
indicate quite a positive or significant interest when, in fact,
there is no interest whatsoever. Some Westerners will deduce
that there is genuine interest, not understanding that saying
'no' is rude for many Arabs - see page 76.

the dignitary, to receive last minute, or new, instructions from that person, and generally to be 'seen'.

There is potential advantage for everyone during the inevitable waiting periods at these gatherings; much networking ensues, much business is conducted. Since all the 'right' people will be present these are ideal moments to mingle, to put across a point of view, and to take soundings. The fact that a foreigner's presentation has had to be missed is of little local consequence when set against the obligation (and opportunities) just described. However, the more-travelled Gulf Arabs are likely, as good hosts, to make contact with the visitors as soon as is convenient, seeking to smooth Western feathers.

The usual suggestion will be that the presentation should be conducted tomorrow, or early the next week "…after the weekend perhaps? Enjoy your time here for a few days. Why rush back to your country? Keep the car – I will send someone to accompany you on an interesting tour tomorrow. The weather is particularly pleasant here at the moment, and I hear that snow is forecast for you at home. I hope to see you on Sunday morning probably, *In Sha' Allah*[12]. Will that be convenient? I will ask my staff to speak to you on Sunday."

Much else that day will have been disrupted for the audience: the Gulf Arabs who should have comprised it will find it odd that the visitors (who purport to be experts) can be so dominated by time, diaries and flight schedules that they become angry and disorientated simply because their presentation has had to be delayed for good reason. "Why don't they understand that we had no choice but to miss their presentation?"

The more experienced Western visitor, knowing Gulf habits, will therefore pretend to be entirely relaxed, and will consider how to join senior members of the 'lost' audience at the airport at once, and thereby, perhaps, conduct useful business. The inexperienced visitor will indicate impatience, while the very foolish will show anger.

'Flexibility' and 'short-notice reaction' are normal components of life for most Gulf Arabs. In the centralised arrangements of most Gulf States, individuals are on call to other more senior Arabs. They can find it odd that visitors from larger and supposedly more developed countries cannot behave as they do. Many Gulf Arabs have no concept, or care, of the pressures, real or imagined, of the visitor's way of life, nor of the financial limitations, budgets and other constraints which surround and dominate most Western companies and government organisations. Westerners, for their part, usually make little attempt to acknowledge or comprehend Gulf Arab lifestyle and therefore cultural clashes are almost inevitable. The 'failed presentation' situation described above is by no means rare – and it always reveals perfectly a wide range of cultural differences which frequently exist between the parties involved – but which, if known about beforehand, can be kept under control.

---

12   Arabic for "If God wills", see page 107.

The working day

This work pattern was probably established because of the effect of the sun on work in the open and before air-conditioning became widespread in offices. In government departments and the armed forces in the UAE for example, in the early 70s, work started at 6.30 am with a breakfast break between 8.30 am and about 9.15 am with all work ceasing at 1.00 pm. Most commercial companies and shops opened again for several hours in the cool of the evening.

The working week

The traditional Gulf working week is from Saturday morning to Thursday lunchtime. A five-and-a-half-day working week is normal. There are increasing variations to this working pattern, e.g. the week starts on Sunday for some Western or international organisations (such as an embassy or a major company), thereby creating the two-day weekend of Friday and Saturday. Working hours can vary considerably: 8.00 am to 1.00 pm Saturday to Thursday, with no work later in the day, may be normal for some government and armed forces departments.

Many of those in government service have found it convenient to combine a public life in the morning with a private, commercial life in the afternoon and early evening. Some companies may add a period in the late afternoon and early evening as well. For many commercial organisations the Western 9.00 am to 5.00 pm arrangement is the norm. It is wise to check the arrangements in each country and in each company.

Telephoning the Gulf on a Friday

Friday is the only certain 'day off' in the Gulf. Those who telephone Gulf expatriates at home on Fridays should be sensitive to this fact for two reasons. The first is the simple reason that most Gulf expatriates need their day off and the majority do not appreciate being disturbed for reasons of work on their 'Sunday'. The second reason is more

subtle: if 'head office' cannot even understand that Friday
is not a Gulf working day, what other more important
confusions and misjudgements are being made about the
nature and pressures of work in the Gulf? "What else are
they getting wrong about me and my work here?"

The rule for 'head office', if work really has to be
conducted with Gulf staff on a Friday, is to apologise first
so that the expatriate can take some minor comfort from
the fact that the person telephoning at least appears to
know about Fridays. It is not unknown for expatriates
deliberately to respond in kind by telephoning their
'head office' colleagues at their homes on Sundays.

9

Language and names

Local language

Arabic is the official language of all the Arab countries of the Middle East. At least some knowledge of the most common words and expressions will prove useful and will make a good impression. English or French is also widely used, particularly in business and commercial circles, in virtually all Arab countries. In Egypt, Saudi Arabia, the Gulf States and Jordan the second language is English. In Syria and Lebanon both English and French are used, while in Tunisia, Algeria and Morocco French is often necessary.

Study of Arabic needed?

Expatriates may well wish to study the Arabic language beyond a basic command of greetings (see below), but this will be more out of cultural interest than for reasons of practical necessity. The study of cross-cultural differences should probably take precedence over language. For example, knowing how to behave in terms of office and personal etiquette, e.g. how to take and decline coffee, deserves more immediate attention than the Arabic language.[13] And knowing of the place of a simple handshake and the use of the words 'As-Salaam Alaykum' (see below) will pay handsomely in terms of establishing oneself in the local business community.

As-Salaam Alaykum

'As-Salaam Alaykum' means 'Peace be upon you'. If said to you, try to respond with the same words backwards:

---

13   See Chapters 10, 11 and 12 on Business Behaviour.

"*Alaykum as-Salaam*" which means 'Upon you peace'. In a
social situation involving males, (in the case of women
see page 33), shake hands, not too firmly, with all nearby
persons, starting with the most senior. These social signals
are highly cost-effective in terms of the minor effort
needed in preparation. However, some fervent Muslims
dislike Westerners using an Islamic greeting and caution
will be needed when in such company.

Saying 'Please' and 'Thank You'

All Westerners expect to use and hear the words 'please'
and 'thank you' frequently in their dealings with others.
Almost all Gulf Arabs will be equally concerned to adopt
similar expressions within their own conversation with
other Arabs and most are fully aware that Westerners will
regard it especially rude if these words are not used. One
Arab said "I know you Western people think that 'please'
and 'thank you' are very important and we do our best to
use them whenever we speak to you, but we take a
different view about the word 'thank you' in particular.
You think it's simply enough to say 'thank you' and that
your obligation for the favour or service is discharged
simply because you have said 'thank you'. We don't think
it's enough – we expect more than words – we expect you
to repay the service or favour in equal measure. And if I
ask to borrow a pencil and I forget to say 'please' – so
what? It was only a pencil I asked for, for heaven's sake –
not the Crown Jewels!"

"I want" and "Give me"

Many Westerners will notice that some Arabs in official
positions, such as traffic police or those at immigration or
customs posts, appear rude and peremptory in their
demands. "Give passport now" and "I want documents"
without the adoption of 'please' and 'thank you'. To many
Westerners this is inexcusably rude English and quick
offence is taken. They therefore fail to recognise that the
Arab involved, often not a Gulf Arab, but an expatriate

Arab from another region such as the Sudan, may not have a command of English above that of functional necessity.

It may be more polite, in Western terms, to say: "May I have your passport, please?" or: "Your documents, please." But, before Westerners become too vexed about what they regard as unpleasant English, they should ask themselves if their own command of Arabic, Farsi, Russian, German, Hindi and French etc. is up to the level of the official addressing them. He is likely to be able to function, politely or not, in all these and other languages, not just English – unlike many visitors and expatriates, particularly Americans and Britons.

Some younger Gulf Arabs, males especially, attending a school or university in the West, for example, can make the social mistake of not adopting 'please' and 'thank you' regularly in their conversation. Their tutors should recognise that this characteristic is not simply a matter of rudeness. "I want Kleenex" may have been the normal, typical and never questioned command in English of a young boy to expatriate third-world servants who were present to look after his every need since birth. Such children have never been exposed to the niceties of polite English and are not accustomed to dealing with staff or minor officials who are not servile. The English of some young Gulf Arabs may become that of their servants in terms of acquired accent, vocabulary and sentence construction. Many Arabs have a good 'ear' for language and speak several, unlike most Western expatriates in the Gulf.

Muslim name sequence

The sequence of a Muslim's name appears complicated for most Westerners but the name should be regarded, for practical purposes, as being in three parts: (1) Own name, (2) Father's name and (3) Family name, e.g. Abdullah bin Mohammad al-Talal (Abdullah, son of Mohammad of the Talal family). This person is known as 'Abdullah'. His own name – his 'given name'– is 'Abdullah'. He is not known as 'Mr Al-Talal' but most well travelled Arabs are used, for example, to hotel reception or airline staff

registering them under their family name only,
e.g. 'Mr A.B.M.A.Talal'. These experienced Arabs are
resigned to this frequent Western mistake and usually
react helpfully if paged or addressed incorrectly. In certain
cases, the adoption of a 'surname' in the Western sense of
the word has become almost normal in business.

Which Mohammad?

Where there are many Mohammads and Abdullahs etc. in
an organisation (which is frequently the case) there can be
confusion. Usually the context or situation indicates which
particular person is under discussion. For example, if both
a doctor and a translator are called Mohammad and the
conversation is about medicine, everyone will know which
Mohammad is meant. Where context or situation does
not remove doubt, the father's name can be added as the
following telephone conversation demonstrates: "Where's
Mohammad?" "Who?" "Mohammad bin Abdullah."
"He is not on his seat[14] – call back in five minutes."

First name usage and its equivalent

Most Arabs will easily sense when personal relationships
with a Westerner have developed to such a point that the
use of the Westerner's first or Christian name may be
adopted as natural and normal. They will know, for
example, that such a point may be reached earlier with
the Americans, later with the French, and somewhere
in between these two nationalities for Britons and other
nationalities.

There is Western difficulty in finding an easy Islamic
equivalent to the 'first name' arrangement. As explained
above, the use of a Muslim's first name does not indicate
any particularly informal status, or any public demonstration that close relationships exist. The first name is

---

14   Many expatriates from the subcontinent will frequently say this in place
     of "He is not at his desk" or "He is not in his office".

already in public use. It is the Muslim's own name. Therefore another mechanism is adopted to indicate informality, certainly in all Gulf countries. This is to call a person 'Abu...' (father of ...). The usual name adopted is that of the first-born son. A simple example is: "When is your next flight back here, John? We really want to keep in touch with you." "In about a week's time, *In Sha' Allah*[15], Abu Mohammad."

His Excellency and Your Excellency

The use of the correct titles and salutations can be a particularly sensitive matter. The level, nature and perceived importance of the use of titles varies between Gulf countries and their personalities. Special care should be taken in all formal written communications. Current, local advice should be sought[16]. Some Arabs (like many people everywhere) can be sensitive to their station and will expect that it be respected. Others prefer to present themselves as informal and accessible persons. As a general rule in the Gulf, it is wise to err on the side of formality, at least initially. The use of 'Excellency' (as in: "We are delighted that His Excellency, the Chairman of the Group of Companies, has been able to join us today to help the negotiations forward") could be used when it has not been possible to check the locally correct salutation, or when it is appropriate to indicate respect to senior figures in the community, or ones who regard themselves as such.

'Shaikh' or 'Sheikh' or 'Shaykh' but never 'Sheek' ?

This title is sometimes spelt as 'Shaykh' or 'Sheikh', but 'Shaikh' is closer to the correct pronunciation, 'Sheek' is quite wrong. A shaikh is addressed as in: "Good morning, Shaikh Mohammad". The title 'Shaikh'

15 Arabic for "If God wills", see page 107.
16 See Sir Donald Hawley's 'Manners and Correct Form in the Middle East' (Michael Russell).

has been also used to show respect to an 'old man revered for age, wisdom, position, learning or saintliness'. At the most formal level, for example at the opening of a major project, one would say: "I have the pleasure to present Your Highness with the keys to this project."

The title 'Shaikh'

In Sir Donald Hawley's 'Manners and Correct Form' (Michael Russell), Sir Donald states: 'The very word 'Shaikh' reveals that in Islam there is no fundamental dichotomy between a temporal and spiritual power. A dictionary definition is 'an elderly, venerable gentleman; old man; elder; chief; chieftain; patriarch; head of tribe; title of the Rulers of Shaikhdoms of the Gulf; titles of scholars trained in the traditional sciences such as clerical dignitaries, members of a religious order, professors of spiritual institutions of higher learning etc; master; master of an order; senator.' In the Gulf, the title 'Shaikh' is used not only by the Rulers of the States and the Crown Princes, but also by members of Ruling Families and, elsewhere, the leaders of tribes. The title 'Shaikh' is often the prerogative of certain families, who have held traditional rule, and such persons may now be found not only in Government but also in the private sector. It is important to check on whom it is proper to address in this way.

10

Business behaviour – the first steps

Months beforehand

Preparation for a business trip to the Gulf should ideally begin a few months prior to the planned date of departure. This is the time when work should be done on all the documentation and presentational matter, to ensure not only the quality of the material, but most importantly, accuracy of all translations[17]. Rarely will there be enough time to prepare thoroughly, but a business trip to the Gulf which is not carefully planned risks ending in expensive failure.

Preparation of documents and presentational material

It is important that all documentation and presentational material is set out impressively and printed or prepared on the highest quality materials. There should be an Executive Summary preferably in Arabic too. Many Gulf Arabs speak excellent English. However, some have trouble with written English and therefore, for this reason alone, if not as a matter of simple respect and politeness to a client, the important sections and summaries should be in Arabic as well as English.

Business cards

These should have English on one side and Arabic on the other. Take care that the Arabic is correct; double check

---

17 Allow five to eight weeks to translate a document the size of this book.

Translations

In some Gulf countries only Arabic is acceptable for certain official documentation. In Saudi Arabia it is not normal to mix English or any other language with Arabic (the language of God for the Muslim) on the same page. Many Gulf nationals are content to see a 'two column' document: English on the left, Arabic on the right. Some Gulf nationals have such a good command of written English that they prefer to see the proposal etc. in English rather than Arabic because they do not wish to rely on the expertise of an unknown translator to present the foreigner's submission accurately

that the printer's translation is in order by showing the proof copy of your card to an Arab colleague before it is printed.

Your translator, not theirs

Proposals in English for significant projects are likely to be examined by a panel of experts or 'Technical Committees' who will report back to a senior personality. Several of those who form such groups will read English well, but others (possibly the majority) will not. Almost all will speak excellent English. The organisation concerned will therefore almost certainly have your proposal translated into Arabic. To ensure that there is no doubt about the accuracy of the Arabic of your proposal it is safest to employ your own translator beforehand whom you know to be competent, and in whom you have full confidence. Leave time for translation to be done; do not rush your translator unreasonably.

Be on time

Do not assume that because many of your Arab colleagues will certainly be late you may also be casual about keeping to time. Arabs know that you are particular about time-keeping and, therefore, if you are late, you might be thought to be casual about the meeting.

Mode of dress and demeanour

As a general rule a business visitor should dress well,
in a good suit and tie, be patient, be on time, expect to wait,
and not be overly demonstrative in personality or mannerism. Businesswomen should dress accordingly but with
slightly lower hemlines than in the West and with the
shoulders and arms covered down to the wrist.

Getting past the gate

For many encounters with large organisations, for
example government or military departments, the first
hurdle is the police or security guard at the entrance.
Even if some kind of appointment or willingness to meet
has been indicated by the department or official
concerned, it does not follow that an effective message to
permit easy entrance will have reached those at the gate.
(The same can be true of any government department
anywhere in the world, not just in the Middle East.)

The security and access arrangements vary from
organisation to organisation, and extra time should be
allowed to gain physical access to the right office. One
helpful idea is always to have to hand the internal

telephone number of your destination office for the security officials so that an internal call can easily be made. Many organisations will expect you to exchange an entrance pass for something important, such as a passport or driving licence, which is reclaimed on departure.

It is effective to phone your contact within the organisation from the car or taxi about 10 minutes before arrival at the gate, inviting him to authorise, or reauthorise, your entrance by calling the guards himself. Your name, or company name, will then be fresh in the minds of those at the gate; this may ease, perhaps speed, the process of gaining entrance. Expect delays; be patient, do not get angry; allow time.

How to behave in an office

Many Arab offices are not private and you may well find others present at what you had assumed would be a private meeting. This is certainly true of the more junior or busy offices, but less so for the more important personalities who will be 'guarded' by large outer offices containing a Secretary (usually male). (The term 'Secretary' is often adopted throughout the Gulf; the function of this person is more that of a Personal Assistant). There will probably be seats along one or more walls of all such outer offices.

Office behaviour: new visitors learn from Gulf Arabs

The visitor, especially during the first few visits, will be expected to identify himself by approaching the desk of the official himself or his Secretary in the outer office. Your approach will be under the scrutiny of all those already seated in the office; it is therefore sensible to behave with quiet confidence at this stage. Nearly all Gulf Arabs can enter any room anywhere with some style, regardless of the relative importance or seniority of those already present, with poise and assurance, and without, apparently, being fazed in the slightest by the occasion or the company.

Gulf Arabs seem able to 'glide' into rooms with straight backs and gentle movements, sensitively observing every-thing and everyone. They do not 'bustle' into rooms: they know how to behave in public, and they seem to know where to go, what to do and how to do it.

Two Western businessmen, horribly new to the Gulf, and utterly unaware of the norms of local behaviour, were seen 'bowing' to the Secretary of an important official from the doorway of a large office. This act, and the ignorance of the Gulf that it indicated, was quickly known throughout the building and beyond; the couple's effective-ness was, in consequence, particularly limited, as they had become a local joke.

A handshake, then sit in the right-hand chair

It would be normal to offer a handshake and to say "*As-Salaam Alaykum*"(see the paragraphs on 'language' on page 50). Take a seat, ideally to the right hand of the official (the right has some importance in the Middle East, as else-where). Such seating may well already be occupied by an earlier visitor who will, if polite, move to a seat further right, allowing you to take that closest to the official. You,

in turn, when the next visitor arrives, should at least make
some indication of willingness to surrender your seat,
but it may be, if that person is a national, that he will insist
that you, as a guest in his country, remain in the more
'important' seat. But your demonstration and awareness
of local behaviour by offering your seat will not go
unnoticed. During your wait, behave as others present
will behave: look and learn from the comings and goings
in the office – competitors may be present and you may
hear something useful.

Coffee and tea in the office

Coffee will inevitably be offered. It is impossible for this
to be refused (see the chapter on Entertaining on page 89)
regardless of how much coffee has already been drunk in
other offices in other places. The coffee will be served,

usually a dash of a somewhat bitter liquid, in a small handleless cup. It is normal to take two cups, perhaps three. Hold the cup in the right hand and do not put it down between sips. Learn beforehand how to decline further cups (by twiddling the cup) as the servant (often the office messenger) will continue to proffer coffee until the signal for 'no more' (the twiddle) is observed. Tea may be served as an alternative to coffee. This will usually be in a small, somewhat thin, glass cup on a glass saucer; with this glass cup and saucer there is no call to employ the twiddle. Such tea is usually very sweet.

The right way

When approaching a doorway in company with an Arab in the Gulf you may find, if he is not already walking on your left side, that he will move to that side at the doorway

itself, insisting that you, as a guest in his country, should go through the doorway first, from the right. For him, the more 'important' person, i.e. the guest, should be on the right and should go through the doorway first. You could show a little resistance to his insistence, reciprocating in the style of "No, no – after you" provided these theatricals are light-hearted and brief. You could say *"min al-yameen"* ("from the right") which should reveal you as something of an Arabist. 'Bluffers' in the Gulf might even deliberately position themselves on the right some way before arriving at the doorway in order to be able to move to the left and defer, as described above at the doorway itself. (Take care: Arabs are good observers of specious activity of any nature; see page 66 concerning the need to be 'genuine' with Arabs.) If you are in company with an Arab in your home ground, try to remember to go through doorways on his left; certainly be second through the doorway. The latter is the proper behaviour of a good host anywhere.

When and how to talk business

The business visitor should be prepared not to come to the point too quickly and should bide his or her time until the moment is right to speak business. When that moment does arrive (and it may take several meetings since Arab office life is often organised on an open-door basis; there will inevitably be many interruptions) it usually occurs quite naturally and without special fanfare or preparation. The visitor should then come to the point promptly, firmly and confidently, dealing only with absolute essentials. However, a number of the younger Gulf Arabs in business have little time for drawn-out pleasantries and, while they will rarely, if ever, speak in a peremptory manner to a stranger, they may themselves seek to bring a conversation to the point quickly – quicker perhaps than their fathers or grandfathers would find normal – seeking, maybe, to indicate their modern outlook and personal exposure to what they may regard as normal behaviour in international business practice.

The first steps

At an initial meeting about three or four well-rehearsed and telling points should be made, drawing heavily on the immediate practical benefits of the offer. Detail should be put across later, perhaps to a specialist committee once the project has received some kind of general initial acceptance by an appropriate personality.

Presentational techniques

Do not start a presentation with, for example, an historical background of the formation of the company, pictures of the founders, last year's performance etc. Instead, do the presentation (in Western terms) upside down: start with the most basic advantages, drawing attention to one or two popular goods or services which have obvious and immediate local benefit. Catch the customer's attention at once, within the first few minutes, no longer; then fall generally silent and await reaction. Gulf Arabs in procurement appointments or private business often have several projects put to them every day and many are boringly presented. Therefore, good preparation is important, not just in presentational technique, but in the construction of an attractive introduction. This latter point – the need for a powerful introduction – may well take considerable research as the circumstances and needs of each country will be different.

Don't tell the client what he wants

Many Gulf Arabs will comment that Western business people can be particularly insensitive in terms of rejecting the wishes of the Gulf customer and in presuming to tell the client what he needs. "No, no, Abdullah, that's not what you need; I don't think you quite understand the full implications of the subject and we are ready to help you, of course." Such condescension would go across badly any-where, but particularly so in the Gulf where condescension does untold damage to personal relationships.

11

Business behaviour – the next steps

Business is personal: family, friends and Muslims first – then strangers

In business matters Arabs usually regard family members as the natural first choice of business partner. For Arabs, in particular, the family unit is a fundamental and powerful alliance, which engenders, and expects, loyalty. It is sensible to promote good business opportunities for, and within, the family. There is less risk of failure and surprise since the personalities will be well known to one another. It is also practical to look to a member of the family for assistance within any large organisation, such as a government department, rather than to bother with any declared official route or documentation; it is simpler to expect the problem in hand to be solved by the family for the family.

Friend – or just a stranger?

If a family member is not available, then business with friends (and then Muslims generally) is the next logical order of choice for most Arabs. Strangers, i.e. the majority of Westerners who visit the Gulf, come a poor, but perhaps unavoidable, third or fourth choice. Since Westerners are not often Muslims, and rarely become part of an Arab family, they can, and should, try to elevate themselves to become genuine friends rather than remaining simply strangers. Arabs (like everyone else) prefer to do business with those whom they know and trust on a personal, friendly basis.

Friendship and instinct

Many Arabs have (or believe they have) special intuition or a 'sixth sense' that guides them towards the correct decision in any matter. This can lead to sudden judgements and instructions that are difficult to dislodge, even in the face of new facts relating to the topic. Many Arabs will often trust their instinct rather than plough through a mass of boring detail. This special Arab sense may or may not exist (and there are many examples when Western 'experts' were, in the long term, proved quite wrong in their advice to their Arab principals). What is certain, in terms of judging people, is that almost all Arabs can quickly notice, and see through, false or shallow 'friendship' sought or maintained simply to advance commercial or other activity. Be 'genuine' in your friendship or relationship; don't 'pretend' with Arabs.

Business and pleasure all together?

Whereas the Westerner usually can and wishes to separate matters of business from matters of non-business, no such separation exists in the minds of most Gulf Arabs. Doing business is perfectly normal at almost any time, particularly when the right moment[18] presents itself. Business may well be conducted after hours and under conditions and in places which may surprise the Westerner. The message is clear: be ready for business at any time, anywhere, just like Gulf Arabs.

Major effort and cost; company regional base

Time, money and effort are needed to establish representation in the Gulf marketplace. This is best done by being resident in the Gulf country concerned, or, but not as effective, by visiting so frequently (perhaps from a company regional base established in, say, Bahrain or

---

18   See page 43 on 'Time and timing'.

Dubai) that one's face becomes familiar. It is not sufficient simply to arrive in-country with an excellent product or service and expect the Arab customer to react quickly and favourably, unless the item in question fills
an instant and urgent need; such opportunities are rare indeed in the Gulf.

Access and bargaining; legal authority to conclude deals

It follows, therefore, that where an individual, such as a resident company representative, or a frequent and trusted visitor, has developed excellent local personal relation- ships, this person has a vital role to play in terms of introducing a total stranger, such as a visiting Chief Executive. The latter, in Arab eyes, will initially have less standing than the resident representative whom they know on a personal basis. But the importance of the Chief Executive in terms of legal capacity to negotiate formally on behalf of the company will not go unnoticed. However, the best possible status for a resident representative is to have personal legal capacity to conclude deals, and be known locally to have such delegated authority. Given that negotiations reach a point of conclusion, probably the most unhelpful and damaging remark a representative can make is: "Well, of course, I cannot personally agree to that price, that's a matter for my manager. I'll ask him to come out to see you." Most Gulf Arabs will regard anyone who has to make such a remark as merely a minor company official, and not really worth bothering with again.

Agenda nibbling

Nearly all Arabs are perfectly at home in a Western office meeting. They observe the meeting's agenda. They note the order and nature of the topics to be handled by the Chair. They can be amused at such stark arrangements, finding it strange that there is an open declaration of what is to be addressed regardless of the mood of those at the meeting, which is not yet known or tested. As Chapter 8 on 'Time and timing' has indicated, many Arabs will

Post-meeting follow-up

The wise visitor or expatriate will, whether in the Chair or not, seek to sum up the essence of any Gulf meeting in a few short, polite remarks at its conclusion so that there are no misunderstandings later. He should follow up with a prompt letter of thanks and a record of what he believes has been decided, perhaps as a precursor to a formal contract if needed. It is best that this letter should be written with urgency, in consultation with 'head office', perhaps in the hotel immediately after the meeting and before departure from the Gulf country.

The letter should be delivered promptly, perhaps with some form of receipt obtained, ideally the next day before memories fade. Some Gulf companies will expect minutes of meetings to be written as a matter of course and, if invited to write the minutes, it is normally best to record only the decisions taken, plus perhaps the general thrust of how these were reached, rather than to name names or to record personal opinions in detail, unless those to be quoted are content to be named and recorded explicitly.

question the wisdom of pressing, or even raising, a point when clearly there is opposition to it, or if the timing is simply wrong.

Are set agendas provocative?

Most Arabs prefer to sound out views on several subjects, to 'graze' an agenda rather than to follow it slavishly, since this allows them to advance their point of view and best interests accordingly. Many will touch on several agenda items, perhaps seeking to return to an earlier agenda item that the Westerners present will regard as finished business. For many Arabs a set agenda can be unhelpful and occasionally embarrassing. Many Arabs will claim to be consensus builders and will seek to avoid causing a loss of face. To invite those at a meeting to vote openly on an issue could be interpreted as provocative.

Testing the water

The best solution is to establish or test the views of all significant personalities before the meeting occurs, since

it may be possible to handle certain matters 'out of court'.
A typical conversation before an important meeting might
be: "Abu Khalifa, would it make difficulties tomorrow
if we raise the matter of staged payments yet again?"
The reply might be: "Sam, those payments are all in hand
anyway so there's no need to raise that subject tomorrow."
The intention to place a subject on an open and formal
agenda can therefore become somewhat of a weapon.
It needs careful handling.

'One-liners' always ready

Effective contact with important decision-takers may be
brief and may occur without warning and quite by chance
(for example while you are walking away from a formal
meeting, in a lift, making farewells at the door, in a car,
i.e. in reasonably private and often the briefest of
circumstances). It is vital to know which 'one-liner'
would serve company interests best at that particular time.
An example of a 'one-liner' is: "This equipment has been
in use with our police forces for years and they love it. May
I show it to yours?" Or: "I hope you will meet my Chief
Executive at the air show reception in the hotel tonight.

Could you spare some time to join us in his room afterwards? I think we are ready to talk about prices now." It is therefore good practice, and good company discipline, to decide and keep these 'one-liners' well up to date and agreed with head office, perhaps on a weekly basis, so that if the moment presents itself the essential and relevant point can be put across confidently.

Loss of temper

Never use mannerisms (such as pointing a finger or raising the voice) which force a direct confrontation or demand an immediate answer or decision, regardless of pressure applied from head office. Above all, avoid a public loss of temper, which will probably end all further discussion or association. A person who has been seen to lose his temper will in future be regarded as an uncultured figure of fun, and must be changed if the project is to go forward. The whole process of developing close and personal relationships will then have to start again.

Silence

Most Westerners find silence embarrassing and will seek to fill a gap in conversation. Many Arabs are wholly unembarrassed by silence and are content, usually, simply to be 'together with friends', savouring companionship by being in another's company. Speech is not always essential on such occasions, and there can be long periods of silence, intermingled with periods of good gossip and story-telling. Many Arabs are aware of, and are perhaps amused by, the stress which silence can cause in Westerners, and it is not unknown for an Arab deliberately to create an embarrassing period of silence when bargaining, perhaps to encourage a concession from the other side. The solution is to be ready to fall silent, and to remain silent.

12

Business behaviour – the final steps

The sport of bargaining

There is a story of a young Arab boy who was asked the question: "What is 2 and 2, Mohammad?" His reply was: "Am I buying or am I selling?" Bargaining is in the Arab blood and Arabs usually regard any opportunity for bargaining and negotiation as good, healthy and necessary sport. And if the other party looks particularly despondent on leaving a bargaining session, so much the better: much kudos accrues to the Arab negotiator from his colleagues and staff.

How to bargain

Most executives will know that the trick is not simply to come down in price, but to restructure the offer in some manner over a series of meetings, which may, for important contracts, take place over two or three (or even more) years. Hold to your price, be firm: "If you want to drop the price to 25 million then of course we have a smaller package for that sum as well, but I thought you wanted the full 30 million version."

All offers and counter-offers must have some element of flexibility within them if the two sides are to agree. Price reduction is the simplest and first example of flexibility, on which most Gulf Arabs will focus promptly. There is, however, a danger in being too flexible over price, for example in opening the price at too high a level in order to be able to come down when under pressure. The following illustrates the pitfall: "So – you started me at 30 million

and you were prepared to conclude at 13 million?
Did you think I could be started at such a figure as 30
million? I wanted your system but it is now unacceptable."

Everyone bargains

Since almost all Arabs enjoy bargaining, it is normal
for them to join in the fun of beating down the price –
any price – or to gain some additional advantage within
the quoted price. The result, for large projects, is that
a number of officials and relatively senior personalities
associated with the project will, almost inevitably, make
some attempt to enter price negotiations, or at least to
make some (probably theatrical) comment whenever
price is mentioned. The secret is to set aside, pleasantly,
all discussion about price except when in company,
usually alone, with the Arab who has power of decision:
"Abu Mohammad, you know I always respect your

judgement and assistance, but I believe Shaikh Abdullah would wish me to keep private my conversations with him about prices. You do understand, don't you? I am to meet him again tonight, as you know. Perhaps he will ask you to be present? – you know we both value your expertise in the project."

Tough but courteous

Most Gulf Arabs will adopt a tough but courteous manner throughout negotiations on price and associated matters. They will expect the other side to behave in a similar way, maintaining personal composure and confidence.

Arab bargaining techniques – pure theatre?

In sharp contrast to the normal politeness and hospitality which the Westerner may expect from most Arabs, it is wise to be prepared for a dramatic change of temperament from the Arab side during bargaining. As already mentioned, most Arabs regard bargaining as natural entertainment and many have honed their techniques to a fine degree. For many, bargaining **is** business: no other business activity (except sponsorship arrangements; see page 78) is more important or more stimulating. Some Westerners can be overwhelmed by the sudden and often powerful theatrical styles involved, especially coming from someone who was apparently, until recently, an example of politeness and hospitality. The following is a notional but typical outburst: "This is a disgrace" (flinging the proposal at the salesperson across the table). "You are a disgrace. How can you possibly be trusted to represent your company with the kind of price you bring to me today? I know your chairman personally – I will tell him of your awful performance here. You are wasting my time – and your company's money – by even bothering to visit me with such a proposal. How can you dare to insult me in this way with such a price! Get out!"

At this point it will be essential to reject, quite strongly but pleasantly, any such outburst. The manner and method will depend on the nature, and strength, of the personal relationship developed between the persons involved at this point, but a clear, even forceful, rejection is needed: "I am sorry you take that line. There will be no need for you to speak to my chairman as I will be reporting immediately to him, and to our sponsor Shaikh Abdul Rahman, about the reception I have received here today. Please accept my apologies if I have misunderstood you. Clearly I have not explained the situation well enough. But this is an important subject – of great benefit to everyone – and I am keen to proceed properly. I want to report that we have made good progress today. Could we try again?"

Senior bargaining techniques

Senior business visitors can probably expect slightly more subtle packaging but nevertheless equally robust treatment: "Mr John, I personally always enjoy our time together, but what you tell me today is, of course, quite hopeless. I am very surprised and indeed angry that you

Variations on the meaning of 'no'

Since there are very many expatriates from the subcontinent in the Gulf, the Westerner should also be ready for this group of expatriates' disinclination to say 'no' or 'I don't know'. This differs, in cross-cultural terms, somewhat from the Arab's reluctance to say 'no' which is more a matter of simple politeness or, perhaps, of bargaining technique. Many from the subcontinent prefer not to answer in a way which might display ignorance of any nature, or to say 'no' since this reply is thought disrespectful. For example, if asked for directions to a particular shop (the location of which they have absolutely no idea), some from the subcontinent will, nevertheless, try to be helpful with directions, invariably pleasantly given. The fact that the directions are subsequently found to be quite hopeless will be frustrating for the Westerner, since the latter, if asked the same question would have said 'Sorry, I haven't a clue; I'm new here myself; you'd better ask someone else' without a thought towards 'politeness' or 'disrespect'.
If challenged later about the directions given, some of those from the subcontinent might excuse themselves, saying 'We only wanted to make you happy'.

have wasted both my and His Excellency your Ambassador's time here today. We both know that the price structure you propose is deceitful and I suggest that you leave me now and go to the airport."

The response needs to be firm: "Shaikh Yousef, I have always admired your English but I cannot believe I just heard the word 'deceitful' from you. There are five separate options: each reflects various quantities and levels of service, and the price of each is therefore different. You seem to be suggesting that I should provide the most expensive option at the lowest price. Clearly this is unrealistic. May I very briefly run through the main options again?"

Concluding the deal

But there must come some clear point when the Arab side recognises that the end of negotiations has arrived and that therefore no further discussion is sensible or possible. At this point the technique is to hold to the two or three options on offer and not to waver from them. Firmness of purpose, put across pleasantly and impersonally, but strongly and very clearly, will be needed at this stage. A walk-out may be necessary. It should, however, be used only at the absolute end of negotiations. Such a point may not be reached until after two or three years' discussion on a major project, possibly even longer.

Saying 'no' is rude

The natural instinct of most Arabs is to be hospitable and welcoming. For many Arabs it is impolite to refuse a guest anything. The guest is king. The guest honours the host by his presence in the host's home and, less so, in the office. The Arab will expect to act as host. The effect in business is that the guest (i.e. the salesperson) must reach the conclusion himself that the goods or services being offered are of no interest whatsoever to the Arab side. This may have been true during the very first sales visit to the Arab country. From the company's point of view, it would have been far more helpful (and cheaper) to have known such a fact earlier so that effort could have been transferred to other markets. For the Westerner that would have been polite. But a typically polite remark from an Arab official during any follow-up visit may well be limited to: "We are still considering the matter. You are always welcome in my country. Do have some coffee. Is your hotel comfortable?" In time the salesperson will no longer visit. The Arab has not had to reach a decision. There has been no refusal. The matter has resolved itself.

Contractual obligations v. personal trust

Most matters are forever negotiable in Arab eyes. Nothing is really concluded, not even if set out in a signed legal contract, freely negotiated beforehand. For an Arab, it is said, friendship and personal trust are more important than legal papers and man-made laws (but never God's law, the *Shariah*; see Chapter 16). Circumstances change, therefore what was once true and agreed is no longer true and can be changed and especially if it brings benefit: "You are my friend and we have known one another a long time. You, of all people, understand our new position, it is difficult now, at this particular moment, to pay you the full contract price we agreed, but we will always look favourably on your company the next time we are looking for suppliers. You, as our friend – we think of you as part of our own family now – can have a word with your people about all this, surely?" However, it would be the height of folly for the Westerner to assume that this friendly 'jam tomorrow' approach works in both directions: Western contractual failure to provide goods or services on time usually means that the Arab organisation concerned will quickly invoke the relevant contract penalty clauses.

The personal touch and strong leadership

The Arab is normally quick to see the personal or family benefit of a certain course of action, and sometimes finds it strange that there should be Western concern for a course of action which does not bring benefit to its proponent, or which does not strike at the heart of the matter. The Arab may feel that some important aspect is missing if the speaker appears to have no personal involvement. Arabs understand perfectly the need to seek personal advantage and benefit, regarding this as a human and natural aspiration, rather than as unreasonable or 'selfish' behaviour. In addition, self-deprecating behaviour or mannerism is often thought odd; most Arabs respect strong leadership and decisive decision-taking.

Local business law

Business in all Gulf countries demands the most careful prior examination of local business law and practice. There are many variations and opportunities. Time and money spent on identifying and arranging the most appropriate legal business status will rarely be wasted.

Selection of an agent or sponsor

Nearly all business arrangements will have at their heart the sponsorship or agency of a national or a national company. There are exceptions relating to certain Duty Free Zones and specific enquiry should be made in each country. A 'sponsor' in a Gulf country does not endorse or provide funds for an undertaking as, for example, a bank might 'sponsor' a sporting event by providing the prizes in return for advertising opportunities. Such 'sponsorship' indeed exists in the Gulf as a normal part of advertising and commerce, but the much more important use of the word 'sponsor' (or 'agency') involves a contractual link between a foreign national or organisation and a national or a national company in the Gulf which is formally registered with a Government department. **The selection of sponsorship arrangements is probably the single most important activity for any company new to the Gulf.** Much local advice and caution is needed. There are scores of examples of unhappy (and happy) partnerships

Business status examples

Commercial Agency, Distributor, General Partnership, Simple Limited Partnership, Joint Venture, Public Shareholding Company, Private Shareholding Company, Limited Liability Company and Partnership Limited by Shares.

between sponsors and those sponsored. These are 'catholic marriages' since separation is not normally simple, regardless of the performance of one side. "It takes two sides to make an agreement, therefore it takes the same two sides to break the agreement" is the usual Gulf legal view of any proposed severance of a sponsorship agreement. The lesson is for both sides to enquire carefully and widely about one another before formalising any business relationship.

"Who is your sponsor?"

As the paragraph above has stressed, the selection of an appropriate sponsor is of such fundamental importance for the success of all business in the Gulf that it must never be hastily arranged. There is, however, a further dimension affecting your relationship with, and the power of, your sponsor. This is the perception of your customers of your (and your company's) standing in the community which flows from that of your sponsor. Many a sales presentation has been interrupted with the words: "Yes, yes, – that's all very fine, but who is your sponsor?" If the name mentioned is particularly impressive, it is not unknown for a deal to be concluded without further delay. Conversely, if the sponsor's name is not particularly well known or is of minor importance, then the next remark from the customer, halting the presentation, might be: "Well, just tell him to come and see me." The essential point is that not only do goods and services on offer in the Gulf have to satisfy need, quality and price, but they also need the 'right' local sponsor and associates.

13

Desert heritage

Clear-sighted

Most Arabs, regardless of background, education or station, can astound Western 'experts' with an uncanny ability to cut through a technical briefing or proposition of the most complex nature. Many are able without difficulty to place a finger quickly on the subjects that matter most in any project.

The demands of the desert

Much of this Arab ability to cut quickly to the bottom line is born of a desert or pearl-fishing heritage in which the practicalities of a harsh and short life – water, food, birth, life, death, danger – took absolute priority. Realities, the proximity of the nearest well, the here-and-now were all that mattered, all the time. Attitudes were (and, in practice, remain) that God controls tomorrow, yesterday is over, and therefore neither is relevant now or can be altered. Only today, now, really matters. Planning and preparation are therefore not well-developed natural Gulf Arab

Modern technology

The mobile phone fits perfectly into modern Gulf Arab lifestyle since it allows friends and colleagues to arrange to meet or to speak internationally 'now' without preparation. Most Gulf Arabs, even those who live mainly in the desert, are singularly unimpressed with modern technology and regard all modern devices as simple tools of assistance rather than as wondrous things. They embrace up-to-date equipment without undue remark – if the item concerned helps and works reliably, it is good; 'how' it works does not matter. This is a good example of the Gulf Arab's ability to cut quickly to the bottom line.

characteristics. Perceptions of time, and obedience to a watch or a diary, are troublesome subjects.

Reputation and 'face'

Bedouin Arabs, nomadic by nature, could not, and did not, collect significant possessions. It was their reputation as hospitable, generous, noble, and brave people that mattered, and still matters. 'Reputation' is a practical alternative to material items in terms of demonstrating personal worth. Many will claim that the best of the Arab comes from this bedouin heritage.

There may be some linkage with a 'loss of face' (page 31) since this has much the same meaning and emotion as a 'loss of reputation'. It could be that the historical and ingrained importance of personal 'reputation' goes some way to explaining why many Gulf Arabs can be particularly sensitive to a 'loss of face', i.e. a 'loss of reputation.'

Memory and rote learning

Most Gulf Arabs have prodigious memories, developed partly because illiteracy was normal in desert society.

Noble Arab legacy

Have a care if you presume to harbour condescending thoughts about Arabs in general. As James Peters in his book 'The Arab World Handbook' (Longman) says: 'Academically they reached new horizons, keeping alive the Greek learning through the Dark Ages and bequeathing us a system of weights and measures and of measuring time, numerals and an alphabet. Their contribution to science is amply evidenced by the numerous Arabic words in the English language such as alchemy, alcohol, alembic, algebra, bismuth, calibre, chemistry etc.' James Peters quotes from Philip Hitti's 'The Short History of Arabs': 'No people in the Middle Ages contributed to human progress so much as the Arabs… Arab scholars were studying Aristotle when Charlemagne and his lords were reportedly learning to write their names. Scientists in Cordova, with their seventeen great libraries, each of which included more than 400,000 volumes, enjoyed luxurious baths at a time when washing the body was considered a dangerous custom at the University of Oxford.'

The ability to recall what was said or done, in considerable detail, often as story-telling, has always been a strength of Gulf Arabs. This deep-seated mental ability has been enhanced by the requirement placed upon many Muslim children to learn by rote and recite the whole Koran or large parts of it.

The business person is therefore well advised not to make casual remarks or to give oral assurances which he or she is not prepared to stand by in the future. Most Gulf Arabs, when it is in their interests, can cheerfully remind you of what you said, where and when. But Arabs can have, like everyone else, selective memories: they are not unknown to pick and choose from their excellent memories whatever suits their purposes.

Camels as road hazards

Although the majority of main desert roads have fencing to prevent camels crossing the road, there are gaps in these fences. Camels sometimes enter these gaps and become trapped outside the fence alongside, or on, the road. The length of the camel's legs means that the bulk of the animal is presented, in any accident, at exactly windscreen height. Do not ignore the danger of camels on roads, especially at dawn and dusk when the colour and texture of the animal blends perfectly into the desert background. If you see cars travelling towards you, or in the distance generally, with hazard warning lights flashing, assume that camels have been seen on the road, outside the fence. Many camels will have their front legs 'hobbled' which means they cannot stray far from the location in which their owner expects them to remain. (It is just possible that there is an etymological link between the English word 'hobble' and the Arabic *habl*, meaning 'rope'.)

The list of desert stupidity

Westerners should visit and perhaps camp in the desert for a few nights if they are to comprehend the kind of life which forms the historical backdrop to the families of many of their Gulf colleagues, and which created many current Gulf Arab characteristics and outlooks.

But all who venture into the desert should take great care and be respectful of the dangers involved. There are many guide-books on this subject and most offer good advice. The most foolish desert activity includes:

- Driving alone in the desert, i.e. not in company with at least one other vehicle.
- Driving in the desert without sufficient water and without a planned route and time of return known to someone else.
- Not knowing the difference between heat stroke and heat exhaustion (see box on page 84).
- Not respecting the dangers of the desert and not taking appropriate advice and equipment.

Heat stroke and heat exhaustion

A person suffering from heat exhaustion will be hot to touch: **clammy, sweating**. A person suffering from heat stroke will be hot: **dry, i.e. not sweating**. This latter person is now at serious risk since the body's temperature mechanism is out of control. This patient will now heat up to the temperature of the day, and may well, therefore, die. Cool the person at once, thereby allowing the body's normal mechanism to reassert itself. Seek urgent medical assistance for anyone in this condition.

- Camping in a *wadi* (valley) at any time, but especially if there is the remotest chance of rain (even 20–30 miles away), which can lead to overwhelming, sudden flash floods.
- Ignoring the major traffic hazard, outside population centres, of the camel (see box on page 83).
- When considering camping, not enquiring into the risk of malaria in the region to be visited (such as the mountains of the UAE in which there can be pools of stagnant water) and not taking the appropriate prophylactics before, during and **after** the trip – and not mentioning such medication when consulting a doctor on any matter in the future.

14

Food

The importance of Arab hospitality is founded on practical grounds and on Islam. Helping someone in need is a good thing to do. It may also lead to reciprocal help for the host at some other time. A favour today begets a favour tomorrow. Historically, the acceptance (and protection) of a stranger in the desert was demonstrated by the offer and acceptance of coffee, water and food. Many personal, social and other indicators were involved. It follows nowadays that if anyone brushes aside the well-established rituals of giving and receiving hospitality as unimportant, this can be taken amiss: even the simple act of refusing coffee in the office can be seen as impolite. The Arab need to demonstrate hospitality and generosity should never be underestimated.

Fasting and eating

During the Muslim holy month of Ramadan, fasting takes place during the hours of daylight. Most people amend their waking and sleeping hours accordingly. It is considered at least very bad manners, and in some countries an offence, to eat or drink or smoke in the sight of a fasting Muslim and in a few countries it may lead to deportation. (See Chapter 18 on Muslim life.)

Eating: right hand

For the majority of Westerners, eating in company with Arabs will be in hotels or restaurants. Table manners will therefore be entirely Western and international. However,

there may be occasions, perhaps in the desert or as a special treat in an Arab's home, when the meal will be bedouin-style, taken communally from a large plate. Goat and/or sheep may be served, cooked whole and presented whole, usually with the head attached, on a large dish on a bed of rice surrounded by various vegetables and other additions. On these occasions, seating will be on the carpet in a semi-kneeling position round the dish. Eat with the right hand by picking up morsels of meat or making small balls of rice and transferring these to the mouth.

Left hand

The left hand has traditionally been reserved for more basic personal toiletry tasks. However, in the modern Arab world there is no need to go into contortions to avoid its use when it is convenient for such tasks as, say, peeling fruit.

The sheep's eye

Part of the West's embedded folklore of the mysterious place 'Arabia' is a belief that all Arab meals lead somehow to the consumption of sheep's eyes at some point in the proceedings. Even though few expatriates have ever faced this delicacy, sheep's eyes usually feature early and embarrassingly in any conversation with those silly towards, and ignorant of, the Middle East.

The majority of visitors and expatriates will unfortunately never meet their Arab colleagues other than in the public rooms and restaurants of business hotels. For those lucky enough to be invited to a traditional meal in the desert and who are indeed offered the eye of a sheep (an extremely rare event, and, for most expatriates, never witnessed) which they do not wish to eat, the simplest action is quietly to leave it or to decline it without special fuss or concern. Such would be the normal behaviour of a guest in a Westerner's home when offered, for example, seafood which the guest cannot consume because of allergic reactions. No host, anywhere, especially in the Middle East where good hospitality is essential and required behaviour (far beyond the norms of the West), will force or chide a guest into eating that which they do not want. In the 1970s one elderly Arab said: "I don't actually like the sheep's eye myself – but I thought my foreign visitors especially liked them, so I have always offered the eyes to them as a matter of politeness."

The goat's tongue

Since lamb and goat are normally served whole, the tongue of either forms a normal part of the traditional meal. It is said that, as a forfeit, those who consume the goat's tongue must, in return, sing a song. In the 1970s one particular adviser quietly hid the proffered tongue under the communal bed of rice in order to avoid eating it. He was observed doing so. (All Arabs are keen observers of all human behaviour and no such ruse could ever go unnoticed.) The host, in due course, leant across, took the tongue from under the rice and, holding it aloft, cried: "Look – we are doubly blessed by God – a goat with two tongues indeed!".

Alcohol and pork

There are special rules concerning alcohol as well as pork (and pork derivatives such as gelatine) which either are not available, or are for sale only under restricted conditions to non-Muslims.

Gulf countries' attitudes to alcohol

Most Gulf Arabs find the habit of some Westerners who drink alcohol to excess to be very strange indeed. The effects of the proscription on alcohol vary between one Gulf state and another and it is necessary to enquire into the arrangements and attitudes of each Gulf country.

15

Entertaining

Invitations

Do not assume that an invitation for a man to dine with a Muslim also extends to his wife or other females, nor, if you invite an Arab to dine with you, that his wife will attend. She will almost certainly not attend unless she and her husband are Westernised and the function is at a hotel and of a type where other Arab wives are certain to be present.

Attendance

Many Arabs, male and especially female, will want to have some good indication of the guest list before accepting, and even then acceptance may not result in attendance. Conversely, your Arab guest may arrive with an unexpected extra friend or two. Buffet dinners, therefore, since they offer flexibility both in numbers and in seating, are far easier to organise than formal set-piece meals. Unless you know them to be reliable attendees, do not rely for the success of the party on too great

Saudi wives' attendance

The likelihood of a Saudi woman attending a business reception or dinner party with strangers is too remote even to consider. There are some Saudi wives who might attend a private foreign function with their husbands provided that there are full reassurances that several other wives will be present, all of whom will be known to one another and all 'Westernised'. These mixed gatherings are most rare.

a proportion of Gulf Arab guests, or you may have a very
dull evening. Arabs tend to leave immediately after a meal
(after coffee) and will normally depart en masse after the
senior Arab guest has gone. Though they will often thank
their host at the time of departure, do not expect to receive
a letter (or phone call) of thanks after the party.

Satiated guests

Arab hosts will expect to press food remorselessly on
guests, and honour will only be satisfied when guests
indicate that not a single morsel more could possibly be
consumed. For a guest to eat everything implies that the
host has been less than generous, an appalling thought
for the good Arab host.

After a traditional meal, hands are washed, coffee
is taken and departures are usually made almost
immediately; the Western habit of continuing

conversation in another room after the meal is not normal. This is, however, not always the case in Oman where conversation can continue into the small hours; much depends on the relationship between host and guests, as is the case anywhere.

Be generous

An Arab, in your house or in your hotel as your guest, may find it strange that you do not ply him unyieldingly with food, coffee or orange juice etc. since that behaviour would be the norm for him, as a host, anywhere. Your Arab guest might also find it odd that you, as host, accept his protestations of 'no more' quite so easily. One Arab said: "I actually did want just a little bit more – but he gave up on me after I had said 'no' only twice. I would have accepted his third attempt – but it never came!"

The sensible Westerner should not attempt to mimic slavishly the behaviour of his Arab hosts, but it will not go unnoticed in terms of your apparent awareness of Gulf Arab habits if you press food, tea, water etc. on your Arab colleagues just a little more than might be normal in Western behaviour, thereby recognising, and complying with, your 'duty' as a host in a Gulf situation. Arabs notice Westerners who seem to be able to demonstrate Gulf norms, and are likely to trust such people more, or earlier, than those who cannot.

Smoking

Many expatriates, especially Egyptians and Arabs from the Levant (see page 7, The Tiers), smoke heavily. Most Gulf Arabs do not. There are Gulf initiatives to restrict smoking and there are a number of buildings in each country, airports for example, where smoking is forbidden, or reserved to special areas only. In some places smokers are required to go outside the building if they wish to smoke. In some Gulf restaurants there are gestures towards 'no smoking' by the earmarking of a few tables to one side of the dining room for non-smokers.

In terms of 'hosting' (see above) there is an additional cross-cultural twist to Western relationships with Arab smokers, as the following comment by a Gulf Arab illustrates: "When I asked him if I might smoke in his house, I was appalled that he said 'no'. I was his guest – how could he possibly say 'no' to me? What a strange man he is!" However, the more sophisticated Gulf Arab will not seek to smoke if it is likely to cause problems for the host, and will seek a convenient place to smoke discreetly.

Entertaining Gulf Arabs in a Western country

Chapter 17 gives advice for companies and organisations preparing to invite Gulf Arabs to Western countries.

16

Law, tax and banks

Law-breaking

Penalties for breaking the law in most Middle Eastern countries can be severe. Serious miscreants may find themselves facing the death penalty. Drug-related activities (consumption or distribution) are treated very, very seriously indeed.

Shariah law

Islamic law is the expression of Allah's command for Muslim society, known as the *Shariah* (the path). *Shariah* is the detailed code of conduct outlining the ways and modes of worship, and the standards of morals and life. It lays down laws that allow judgement between right and wrong.

Nature and significance of Islamic law

The science of ascertaining the precise terms of the *Shariah* is known as *fiqh*, which means 'understanding'. In classical form the *Shariah* differs from Western systems of law in two principal respects. Firstly, the scope of the *Shariah* is much wider than Western systems since it regulates man's relationships not only with his neighbours and with the state (which is the limit of most other legal systems) but also with God and man's own conscience.

The second difference is the Islamic concept that *Shariah* law is an expression of divine will. *Shariah* law became a rigid and static system, unlike secular Western systems that grow out of society and change with the evolving circumstances of that society.

Sources

> The first two sources of the *Shariah* are the Koran and
> the *Hadith*. Other sources include *ijtima* ('consensus'
> of the Prophet's disciples) and *qiyyas* (measurement or
> mental reasoning). The Koran is divine, every word is
> from Allah. The *Hadith* is the record of the Prophet
> Mohammad's (PBUH)[19] sayings, conduct and behaviour
> preserved by those who were present in his company,
> or by those to whom such memories were handed
> down by these first witnesses.

The sections

> *Shariah* law has five main sections. These are:
> Penal Law, Transactions Law, Family Law, Divorce Law,
> Succession Law.

The Westerner and the *Shariah*

> The non-Muslim expatriate, however, given that he
> or she behaves in a way which is acceptable in general
> terms under laws of the West, need have no fear of the
> *Shariah* since the court is less concerned with commercial
> or contractual matters or with traffic offences not involving
> death, injury or alcohol. There are other, secular,
> mechanisms and codes for dealing with 'modern' activity
> such as air or sea navigation, corporate law, and banking
> practice, but a complainant can always invoke the *Shariah*
> which remains available for almost any matter.

The quiet approach is best

> Families of Westerners accused of major offences
> in the Gulf will not gain much by calling for, or achieving,
> strident Western publicity of the situation, in order to raise

19   See box on page 108

the profile of the case. Gulf officials, and those in senior authority, resent the usually ill-informed and sensationalist condemnation of their judicial process and are wearied by the widespread and long-standing ignorance of the West in such matters. Sensible family members will therefore work quietly with their diplomatic representatives to achieve an acceptable solution, the best usually being discreet departure, or, although not as satisfactory, deportation from the Gulf on completion of a minor sentence. Those in power in the Gulf are more disposed to help those who do not exacerbate the situation (which may already be a matter of embarrassment to them) by making sensationalist public protests. The authorities may simply wish that the accused should depart quietly and unseen on the next available aircraft.

International publicity is rarely helpful, especially as a first reaction. Promoting publicity may be tempting to the relatives of the accused, but they are likely to be ignorant of the legal checks and balances that exist in all Gulf countries, and early clamour usually has the opposite of the desired effect since it means that (1) the authorities will now be determined that the external and probably arrogant interference shall be opposed and (2) – and more importantly – the authorities will be 'known to know' of the case, which cannot now be conveniently ignored or treated privately and quietly in a way that suits all parties. Instead, the authorities will now have to be seen to take full, proper (i.e. Islamic) and public action, which may limit their options. Noisy protest is almost never the best first option when dealing with any Gulf situation or personality. (The flexibility to 'ignore' a situation is important and useful in the Gulf. As a general rule, do nothing that 'cannot be ignored'; see the box on page 15)

Tax

The Middle East has a long tradition of attracting expatriates to work in its colossal petro-chemical, oil and gas industries. Job opportunities are plentiful, wages can be high, and tax systems are normally among the most lenient in the world. In some parts income tax is non-existent although there is talk of taxation being introduced from time to time in various countries. There is some local taxation such as the municipality taxes in the UAE that are applied to hotel bills. Specific taxation advice must be taken.

Banks and banking; probate

Most countries in the Middle East have a modern banking system but the arrangements will differ somewhat between countries. Banking is not normally a major difficulty for companies and individuals to address as part of their preparation for business in the region. However, Direct Debit and Standing Order arrangements are not in widespread use in the Gulf, and utility payments, such as those for the telephone or electricity, are usually settled by cheque, or cash.

For couples, it is wise to have a joint personal bank account which operates on the signature of either spouse. On a husband's death, the release of funds from a single account, in a husband's name only, will be more difficult and will be delayed until a *Shariah* court has granted probate. For a widow, the certification of her entitlement to the funds in the account may have to be sworn to the court by two males, probably required to be Muslims.

Islamic banking

Islamic banking[20] is based on teachings from the Holy Koran which are clear about the prohibition of *Riba* which is sometimes defined as excessive interest. However, Muslim scholars have accepted the word to mean any fixed or guaranteed interest payment on cash advances or on deposits. Several Koranic verses expressively admonish the faithful to shun interest.

---

20   The following information is from Mohammed Aslam Aseem's article in the Gulf News Business Section, 14 June 1997.

The prohibition on paying or receiving fixed interest is based on the Islamic tenet that money is only a medium of exchange, a way of defining the value of a thing. It has no value in itself and, therefore, should not be allowed to give rise to more money via fixed interest payments simply by being put in a bank or lent to someone else.

The human effort, initiative and risk involved in a productive venture are more important than the money used to finance it. Islamic economics is based on the belief that the provider of capital should share the risks of business ventures.

17

Arranging a visit for Gulf Arabs to a Western country

Preparation for the visit

For companies whose business activity in the Gulf has developed to such a point that a visit by a delegation of Gulf Arabs to the factory or similar establishment is appropriate, the following paragraphs may be helpful. Most Gulf Arabs have considerable international experience and are well travelled. They therefore need little personal preparation for a business trip to the West. Many own properties in the UK, the USA, Spain and elsewhere. Most are fully aware of the nature and culture of many nationalities and are well prepared for business with, and in, the West.

A three-day week

On the assumption that a period of one week has been generally agreed for the visit, Sunday will probably be the most convenient day for the delegation's arrival; it will give them the opportunity to be ready for work on the Monday after a night's rest. The most convenient time for departure is probably the latter part of Thursday; Friday is also a satisfactory day but not as popular as Thursday. Thursday, or Thursday afternoon, is usually set aside as a time for shopping or as private time before departure, perhaps on an overnight flight back to the Gulf. The effect, for the delegation, is that Monday, Tuesday and Wednesday will be regarded as the normal working days, while the balance of the days during the visit 'week' are usually not.

Evenings free?

Many Gulf Arabs hope not to undertake 'work' in the evenings and, in this context, attendance at dinners or receptions organised by companies is regarded as 'work.' Attendance at an event or function early in an evening is likely to be quite popular since it is unlikely to spoil private Arab gatherings arranged for later in the evening. Most Gulf Arabs have many friends and associates in capital cities (particularly in the summer months) and it is normal for them to wish to meet one another if possible. Dining with, or meeting, Arab friends is much more attractive than dining on unusual, i.e. Western, food with business strangers. Arab gatherings usually occur in the evenings and may well involve calls on members of Gulf ruling families if present in-country. Such calls will be almost a matter of obligation and the business programme should be flexible enough to permit it.

Visit escort

It is best to appoint one person from the company or organisation who is already known personally to at least the leader of the delegation, such as the Gulf representative of the company, to accompany the group from arrival until departure. It is not normally wise to hand over the delegation from one company personality to another as the visit progresses. The escort should regard being in close company with a senior Arab personality, and others in the delegation, as a particularly useful opportunity to enhance personal relations, and to conduct business when appropriate. If a 'stranger' has to be appointed as escort, then that person should ideally have some prior knowledge of Gulf Arab culture. Some companies deliberately nominate a person who is about to assume a Gulf appointment, or perhaps someone who is to visit the region frequently, or is to take up Gulf residence on behalf of the company. The delegation's visit presents a perfect opportunity to make friends.

The task of the escort

The task of the escort is to be on hand to the delegation, linking the components of the visit programme smoothly and solving problems such as those of transport and other changes to the plan. A mobile phone (and perhaps also a pager, as back-up) will be absolutely essential. The escort, almost certainly, should stay in the delegation's hotel, or be very close by, helping the delegation by explaining and confirming the next stages of the programme as it unfolds and advising the delegation of the personalities it is to meet (or has met).

The escort should become a friend to the delegation, giving warning ahead to the company of the wishes of the delegation, and vice versa. Such wishes may only emerge from the delegation at the very last moment: "Harry, could we not go to Scotland today but go to the factory in Marseilles instead? Could your Chairman meet us there rather than in Scotland – will that be a problem? And my brother is arriving at Heathrow tonight so I can't attend the company reception at the Dorchester after all and I'll have to leave with him for Morocco early tomorrow. You do understand, don't you? – and you will explain to your people that he is my brother?" (See page 65 concerning 'the family'.)

Or, from the escort: "John, I've just seen that they're going to present the MD with an enormous silver palm tree – have we got something impressive for the MD to present to them when I bring them up to meet her in half an hour?"

Escort to withdraw – but not the driver(s)

The discerning escort will know when the delegation wishes to have time to itself and will withdraw accordingly. However, the delegation will appreciate the continued presence of company cars and drivers, which should be made available to them for private use. The escort should not feel obliged to entertain or shadow the group all the time; most Gulf Arabs have much experience of capital cities and need no nannying.

Which hotel – old or new?

Some Westerners believe that Gulf Arabs may wish
to be accommodated in, or to visit, hotels and places
of historic interest during their visit. However, most
Gulf Arabs tend to prefer modern and well equipped
international standard hotels and it is usually best to
select a hotel which has experience of international
clientele, ideally with a kitchen and room service staff
experienced in serving Arab guests.

Who pays for what? Two accounts?

Unless the company is prepared to pay the whole of the
visiting delegation's expenses, regardless of cost, it is
sensible to set out clearly, at the time of the invitation,
the arrangements for meeting the costs of the various
elements of the visit. For example, many organisations
will offer to pay for either on the one hand the airfare,
or on the other, in-country food, accommodation and
transport. This division is normally acceptable to both
sides and is often the reciprocal arrangement offered to

official Western or international delegations invited
to visit Gulf countries.

Given that the delegation is content to pay its airfares,
the prudent company or organisation will write to the
hotel concerned requiring that there be two accounts for
each member of the delegation: one account for food
and accommodation not to be charged to the individual,
and another to be a personal account, chargeable to the
individual as a contract between hotel and guest, formal-
ised at check-in. Major hotels are accustomed to such
split accountancy arrangements. Incidentals, for example
long-distance telephone charges and shopping, therefore
become a cost for the hotel to recover at check-out.

Correspondingly, for official visits to the Gulf where
alcohol is available in hotels it is not normal for alcoholic
drinks to be chargeable to the host country, e.g. from
the mini-bar as part of 'accommodation', nor, in theory,
wine with a meal as part of 'food'. The secret, for everyone,
whether visitors from the Gulf or to the Gulf, is to be quite
clear before, and at the start of, the visit about payments.
The escort can play a useful part in this matter.

Surely they know about pork and alcohol?

There is no guarantee that even the most experienced
caterers or hotels will not offer pork-based food (or food
prepared with alcohol) to Muslims by accident. Few food
and beverage managers or senior chefs would ever make
such gross mistakes themselves as all are fully aware of
every possible international culinary and dietary
restriction and preference. The problem is normally
much closer to the point of delivery, for example if the
task of providing food for a reception has been carelessly
sub-contracted, e.g. 'Provide 200 canapés for a reception
in Room 213 at 7.00 pm – usual selection,' or if there has
been a lack of supervision or a last-minute problem in
the kitchen requiring the replacement of part of the menu.
It is therefore desirable to check that even the most
illustrious hotels, caterers, etc. do not place pork or
alcohol-based products on the same plate as other food.

Separation

Pork can still be served to non-Muslim guests, but it
should be prepared in a separate kitchen and be
presented on a separate plate, and be clearly marked
as pork, or pork-based. Alcohol can also be served,
unless the delegation is known to be led by, or to
include, someone who may be offended by this;
discreet enquiry should always be made as part of
the visit preparation, or from the escort. There
should, of course, be plenty of non-alcoholic drinks
on hand as well.

The essential point is that both guests and hosts
should be able to choose whatever they wish to
consume and have a pleasant time together; for
the Muslim this means reassurance that the plate or
glass presented does not contain something unpleasant
or forbidden. Food offered buffet-style (with dishes
containing pork or alcohol clearly marked), rather than
served formally at table, is often the simplest solution
since it permits choice.

Prayers and prayer rooms

Most Muslims will wish to have the opportunity to pray at
several times during the visit period. The most devout will
expect to do so five times each day (see Chapter 18 on
Muslim Life). The majority of Muslim business visitors
will probably pray privately in their hotel rooms and the
topic need not become a special subject to be addressed
by those organising the visit.

Since Muslims find the act of praying absolutely
normal, there should be no need for the activity to be given
any special prominence in terms of conversation or in the
allocation of 'special rooms'. The essential point to
establish is whether the group contains any particularly
religious person(s) and, if so, whether the prayer times
create any particular problem in terms of the visit
programme. If there happens to be a natural break in the
programme close to one of the prayer times and there is

also a room conveniently available (without tables or chairs is best) the group may well wish to pray together.

There is no need for any announcement or special highlighting in the programme; a quiet word to the leader of the group by the escort that the room is available nearby is all that is needed.

18

Muslim life

Islamic States

The Organisation of the Islamic Conference (OIC) is one of two pan-Islam organisations[21]. The Charter of the OIC is to promote Islamic solidarity and many other topics among member states who currently include[22]:

Afghanistan	Guinea-Bissau	Pakistan
Albania	Indonesia	Palestine
Algeria	Iran	Qatar
Azerbaijan	Iraq	Saudi Arabia
Bahrain	Jordan	Senegal
Bangladesh	Kuwait	Sierra Leone
Benin	Kazakhstan	Somalia
Bosnia and Herzegovina	Kyrgyzstan	Sudan
	Lebanon	Surinam
Brunei	Libya	Syria
Burkina Faso	Malaysia	Tajikistan
Cameroon	Maldives	Tunisia
Chad	Mali	Turkmenistan
Comoros	Mauritania	Turkey
Djibouti	Morocco	Uganda
Egypt	Mozambique	United Arab Emirates
Gabon	Niger	Uzbekistan
Gambia	Nigeria	Yemen
Guinea	Oman	

21 The second is the World Muslim League, with its headquarters in Makkah. It supports Islamic causes.
22 Source: Web site http://www.sesrtcic.org

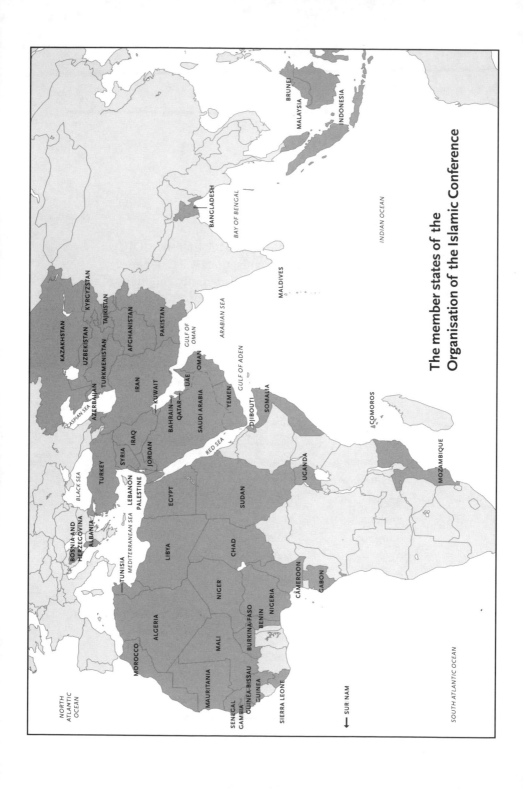

The member states of the
Organisation of the Islamic Conference

Level of study of Islam

It is sensible that expatriates in the Gulf comprehend the outline and power of Islam if they are to spend pleasant and productive time in harmony with their Muslim colleagues and friends.

The comments that follow concentrate, almost exclusively, on those features of Islam that affect, or will be noticed by, non-Muslim Westerners during their times in the Gulf. Much has therefore been left unsaid.

Definition and background

Islam is the religion revealed to the Prophet Mohammad PBUH (see box on page 108) in what is now Saudi Arabia between AD 610 and AD 632. He was born in Makkah in AD 570 and died in Medina in AD 632. There are said to be at least 950 million Muslims worldwide. Literally translated from the Arabic, Islam means 'committed to the will of God' and a Muslim (also spelt Moslem)[23] is 'one who submits'. A Muslim's faith can be intense; the submission to the will of God is total.

God's will

A Muslim believes that God's hand is present in every occurrence on earth. Nothing can happen without God ordaining it. Muslims often proclaim that such and such will happen 'if God wills' (*'In Sha' Allah'*) or that an occurrence was the will of God (*'Ma Sha' Allah'*).

Code of conduct

Islam not only contains a powerful and unequivocal spiritual message but also sets out a comprehensive code

---

23   Take care not to pronounce the 's' as a 'z' since this creates the sound 'Muzlim', which comes close to the Arabic word 'Zulm', i.e. 'Harm' or 'Evil'.

> **Peace Be Upon Him (PBUH)**
>
> In Muslim circles mention of the Prophet Mohammad (PBUH) in speech or in writing must be followed by the words 'Peace be upon him' (usually shortened to 'PBUH') as the mark of respect commanded by the Koran.

of conduct. The Koran, the Holy Book of Islam, lays down a complete set of rules covering every aspect of human behaviour. The rules are clear and every action in life is classed as either Obligatory, Recommended-Approved[24], Neutral, Disapproved or Forbidden. Islam, therefore, can be said to govern a Muslim's whole way of life and thought.

Pillars or Duties of Islam

The Five Pillars (primary duties) of Islam are:

- Bearing Witness to the Oneness of God and to His Prophet, Mohammad (PBUH).
- Prayer, five times a day.
- Alms-giving ('purifying dues') to the poor, the destitute, etc.
- Fasting during the holy month of Ramadan.
- Pilgrimage to Makkah at least once in a lifetime for those who can afford it.

Islam everywhere

Islam is everywhere in Arab daily life. Religious texts are to be seen in houses, offices and elsewhere. Worship is performed openly in public with a complete lack of self consciousness and takes priority over most other activities. There is constant reference to God and His Prophet in public or formal speeches (whatever the subject), on the radio and in the newspaper. Most letters are headed with the words: 'In the name of God, the Merciful, the Compassionate'.

---

24   Alternative words for the same category of rule, in Arabic *mustahab*.

After the Prophet

After Mohammad's (PBUH) death in AD 632, Abu Bakr[25] was elected *Caliph* (successor). He died two years later after a brief illness. He was succeeded by his nominee, Umar ibn al-Khattab, as the second *Caliph*, who died in Medina in AD 644. A council (the *Shura*) elected the new *Caliph*. The main candidates were Ali ibn Abu Talib[26] and Uthman ibn Affan[27]. The *Caliphate* went to the latter, who ruled the Muslim state from AD 649 until his death 12 years later, at which time the former was elected *Caliph*. These two *Caliphs* and others form the backdrop to the two main Islamic denominations to be noticed today. Westerners may wish to enquire further into the rich culture and beliefs of both denominations as part of their preparation for, or life in, the Gulf states when the subdivisions of the denominations, and their effect, will be discovered.

The Sunnis The *Sunnis* draw their lineage from the election of Uthman ibn Affan as *Caliph*. '*Sunnah*' in Arabic embraces the 'way' of the Prophet and his reported actions and sayings.

The Shiites Ali ibn Abu Talib's supporters formed the *Shi'at Ali*, 'Party of Ali', from which *Shiite* or *Shi'a* derives.

The Muslim calendar

The Islamic calendar dates from the *Hejira*[28]. In Western terminology Muslim years are suffixed 'AH' (Anno *Hejira*: in the Year of the *Hejira*). 1 AH corresponds to 622 AD. The *Hejira* year is based on lunar cycles and is about 11 days shorter than the Western Gregorian year (Anno Domini, AD), which is based on solar cycles.

25 The Prophet's closest friend and father of his wife Aisha.
26 The husband of the Prophet's daughter, Fatima.
27 A member of the more distantly related *Umayyad* clan and a rich and influential member of the group.
28 The 'migration' (*Hejira*) of the Prophet Mohammad (PBUH) from Makkah to Medina.

Months

Months are either 29 or 30 days:

1st month	*Muharram*
2nd	*Safar*
3rd	*Rabi' al-Awwal*
4th	*Rabi' al-Thani*
5th	*Jumad al-Awwal*
6th	*Jumad al-Thani*
7th	*Rajab*
8th	*Sha'ban*
9th	*Ramadan*
10th	*Shawwal*
11th	*Dhul-Qa'dah*
12th	*Dhul-Hijjah*

Fridays

Friday is the day of congregational worship. In most countries the official holiday period is from Thursday to Friday, but increasingly Friday and Saturday are chosen as the weekend period.

Prayers and their observance

Muslims are expected to pray five times a day. Observance varies throughout the Middle East. In Saudi Arabia shops will shut and all forms of work cease. Supermarkets will shut their check-out counters and shoppers will be unable to leave during prayer times, which last about 30 minutes. In other parts of the region, work will continue largely as normal, it being left to the individual Muslim to decide whether or not to pray, often openly in public or in a prayer room set aside by the company or organisation for the purpose.

It is best for non-Muslims not to show any special interest in those praying; staring is somewhat rude, although most Muslims will claim that praying is so utterly normal that there can be no possibility of

Prayers on aircraft and in hotels

On certain aircraft, the *qibla* is indicated by an arrow shown on a special electronic display which continuously points to the direction of Makkah throughout the journey. The display often gives the time of prayers at Makkah (and often the prayer times appropriate to the departure and destination locations of the aircraft as well). Some Muslims will pray in an open space on board the aircraft. In most hotel rooms in the Middle East (and in many international hotels elsewhere) the *qibla* is indicated by an arrow decal, normally green in colour, fixed to the top of the bedside table or to the ceiling, with its arrow pointing towards Makkah so that the correct personal orientation for private prayer can be known.

embarrassment whatsoever. It is polite for non-Muslims not to place themselves directly between those praying and Makkah; Muslims face the direction of Makkah (*qibla*, see box) in order to pray.

Prayer timings

The precise timings for prayer vary with the apparent cycles of the sun daily throughout the world and are usually published in local newspapers and other media of the Middle East. Timings will change by a few minutes or seconds each day. For example, the prayer timings published for the UAE on three dates for Dubai were as shown below. Purists would add four minutes for Abu Dhabi, and deduct four for Ras Al-Khaimah and six for Fujairah:

	23 August 1997	1 February 1998	4 June 1998
(1) *Fajr* (Dawn)	0437	0542	0409
(–) *Shuruq* (Sunrise)	0557	0702	0529
(2) *Dhuhr* (Midday)	1226	1237	1222
(3) *Asr* (Afternoon)	1557	1545	1547
(4) *Maghreb* (Sunset)	1848	1806	1908
(5) *Isha* (Night)	2018	1936	2038

> **Dawn, sunrise and the black and white threads**
>
> Fasting (page 114) starts when one can see the difference between a black and white thread at dawn. Soldiers call this 'first light'. Sunrise, and the end of the pre-dawn repast (*suhar*), is when the sun's aurora is first seen in the East.

Five prayers per day – why six shown in the newspapers?

Dawn prayers are best observed at dawn itself. Many Muslims will agree that the dawn prayer has special significance. The reason that the newspapers show the time of *Shuruq* is that sunrise is the latest time by which the dawn prayer should be undertaken.

The call to prayer

The loudspeakers of most mosques will call the faithful to each prayer time. New expatriates searching for accommodation near mosques should bear the certainty of the dawn and other calls to prayer in mind when deciding where to live.

> **Technology and the call to prayer**
>
> *The Mikat*
>
> A small electronic Belgian device, the Mikat, programmed for some 140 major cities, calls the faithful to prayer and shows the direction of Makkah. This is a particularly helpful device for Muslim business travellers and for Muslims in foreign countries where the call to prayer from the loudspeakers of mosques is not appropriate.
>
> *Prayer times from the net*
>
> The following web sites include Islamic programmes to allow searches which find the daily prayer times at many locations worldwide at various times, months and years:
>
> http://www.uwm.edu/cgi-bin/bashir/salat.cgi
> http://www.solat.net

The words of the calls to prayer and their meaning

The sequence and repetition of the seven calls to prayer (eight for the dawn prayer) are shown below:

1 *Allaahu akbar.* (God is the greatest *or* God is very great.)
2 *Allaahu akbar.* (God is the greatest/is very great.)
3 *Allaahu akbar.* (God is the greatest/is very great.)
4 *Allaahu akbar.* (God is the greatest/is very great.)

1 *Ashhadu an laa illallah Ha-illaah.*
  (I testify that there is no god but God.)
2 *Ashhadu an laa illallah Ha-illaah.*
  (I testify that there is no god but God.)

1 *Ashhadu anna muhammadan rasuulu-llaah.*
  (I testify that Mohammad is His messenger.)
2 *Ashhadu anna muhammadan rasuulu-llaah.*
  (I testify that Mohammad is His messenger.)

1 *Hayya ala as-salaah* (Come to prayer.)
2 *Hayya ala as-salaah* (Come to prayer.)

1 *Hayya ala al-falaah.* (Come to salvation.)
2 *Hayya ala al-falaah.* (Come to salvation.)

Dawn prayer call only:

1 *As-salaatu khayrun min al nawm.* (Prayer is better than sleep.)
2 *As-salaatu khayrun min al nawm.* (Prayer is better than sleep.)

All prayer calls conclude:

1 *Allaahu akbar.* (God is the greatest/is very great.)
2 *Allaahu akbar.* (God is the greatest/is very great.)

1 *Laa illaah illa allaah.* (There is no god but God.)

RAMADAN

The holy month

Ramadan lasts a full lunar month. All adult Muslims are required to abstain from food, drink and tobacco and certain other pleasurable pursuits between sunrise and sunset. This can be a great burden, especially in summer, and hours of work are shortened accordingly. The extent of abstinence depends on how strict the individual Muslim considers himself to be.

Ramadan nights

Nights become alive during Ramadan: shops are open, there is a bustle generally and traffic on the roads can be heavy into the small hours.

Fasting

Fasting is compulsory for Muslims during Ramadan except for the young, the aged, the sick, nursing or pregnant women and travellers on long journeys. However, if an able-bodied adult misses a day (or days) of fasting during travel or sickness, fasting (in compensation) for the same number of days missed must take place later. Naturally one should show consideration and not eat, drink or smoke in public or in the presence of a Muslim during daylight hours. It is a punishable offence to do so in public in some Arab countries.

Thoughts and deeds

In addition to fasting, the good Muslim will also try to avoid all evil thoughts, actions, demands and wrong-doing, some of which can annul the fast. Lying, back-biting, slander, a false oath and a 'glance of passion' all annul the fast.

A Western woman should, as always in the Gulf, dress modestly, i.e. she should not wear a short skirt or have bare arms. It is singularly insensitive to wear such clothing during Ramadan.

To be avoided are: indecent or dishonest talk, and hostile and hypocritical behaviour. The fast, in calling for the exercise of patience, serves to inculcate the virtues of endurance, tolerance, and respect for fellow human beings.

Breakfast

The fast is broken each day at sunset by the consumption of water plus, perhaps, a date. This minor 'break-fast' is known as *iftar* and is followed by the *Maghreb* prayers and a major meal. Most Muslims will then call on (and/or receive) family, friends and associates in their homes. These visits and gatherings can last into the small hours.

Tiredness

Most Muslims become tired in the day and increasingly so as the holy month advances. It is therefore both polite and sensible to show understanding of the pressure of Islamic life (contentedly borne by Muslims) during Ramadan, making allowances by, for example, shortening training programmes or seminars, particularly in the last weeks of the month. Many Muslims in the Gulf will not be found in their offices other than for brief periods towards the end of the morning, if at all.

Visits and calls

Many expatriates will call on their Arab colleagues during Ramadan evenings and nights. Even though most Arabs are happy to deal with matters of business at any time, it would be somewhat clumsy (but by no means impossible) to guide conversation to business during a Ramadan call. This is a time to visit colleagues, friends and family. Such calls are rarely unproductive and there may well be a brief moment when business can be mentioned privately.

When does Ramadan start?

For many non-Muslim expatriates and visitors the fact that the start (and end) of the month of Ramadan does not seem to have fixed dates is always confusing. But, since the Muslim year is lunar-based (see page 109), a new moon marks the start of each month. For the start of the holy month of Ramadan it has, in the past, been customary and necessary for an actual sighting of the new moon to be properly reported to appropriate Islamic authorities by acceptable Muslim witnesses so that the commencement of the month can be joyfully promulgated throughout the Muslim world. There may, however, be some variance in the official announcement of the start of Ramadan by each Gulf state.

When does Ramadan end?

The sighting of the new moon marks the end of Ramadan which is the start of the two or three-day *Eid al-Fitr* holiday and the beginning of the following month, *Shawwal*. As the start of Ramadan, its end can vary by a day or so in different Muslim countries. Local media will announce, perhaps only one day beforehand, the *Eid* holiday period for government personnel, which the private sector will then generally follow. For practical purposes you should simply note when the period of Ramadan and its *Eid* occurred last year and assume that the same period will be 10 or 11 days earlier in the current year.

Eid al-Fitr

Some Muslims will say that *Eid al-Fitr* corresponds in importance for Muslims to the importance of Christmas for Christians. The wish for, and pleasure of, families to be together at the happy time of holiday and feast are much the same. Those who are providing training or other assistance for Muslims on courses outside the Gulf (and without doubt within the Gulf) should try, if at all possible, to grant a period of holiday for *Eid al-Fitr* if this falls conveniently in the programme.

One wise Arab, on hearing that a Western organisation proposed a date for a meeting which was almost certain to clash with the *Eid*, reacted: "No, that's not a particularly good date for me – how about 25 December instead? I take it that will be OK?"

PILGRIMAGE

Duty of pilgrimage

Pilgrimage (*Hajj*) is one of the five pillars of Islam. Muslims are required to visit Makkah, and its associated holy places once in a lifetime if at all possible. Those Muslims who complete the pilgrimage are entitled to be known as *Hajji*. The pilgrimage takes place during the month of *Dhul-Hijjah* and lasts some ten days.

It is not unusual to be approached by colleagues or friends before they leave for their pilgrimage to confirm that no misunderstandings exist. This is to ensure that there are no outstanding disputes which might stand in the way of a successful pilgrimage. One should simply confirm the position and wish them well.

Saudi Arabia, the birth place of Islam and the country guarding two of the three holy places of Islam, Makkah and Medina (the third being Jerusalem), has a special burden as annual host to the enormous numbers of visiting Muslims. Travel to Makkah, once overland by pilgrim caravans, is now normally by air. Saudi Arabia has had to impose restrictions by national quota in order to bring some order and control to the huge crowds of visitors. Only Muslims may enter Makkah.

FESTIVALS

Eid al-Fitr

As mentioned before, the 'festival of breaking the fast' marks the end of Ramadan and takes place on 1 *Shawwal* (the 10th month) and the following two days. *Eid al-Fitr* is a time of great joyfulness and celebration. Visits are exchanged with friends and relations and children are given gifts of money or clothing. You should say "*Eid Mubarak*" on 1 *Shawwal* to greet a Muslim on the occasion of the *Eid* holiday. A special mandatory payment (*zakatul*) is also paid by Muslims just before

this time; it is a specific amount of food or money
sufficient to provide a meal for someone in need.
Another feature of the festival is a special additional
congregational prayer, often at a particular mosque only
set aside especially for this annual event. *Eid al-Fitr* is
sometimes known the 'Small *Eid*' (the larger being
Eid al-Adha, see next paragraph).

Eid al-Adha

The 'festival of sacrifice', *Eid al-Adha*, which is the greater
of the two main festivals, falls on 10th *Dhul-Hijjah* and
the following three days. It commemorates the time
when Ibrahim[29] (Abraham) was willing to sacrifice his
son Ismail as an act of total devotion to God. In the event,
a sheep was sacrificed in Ismail's stead as a symbol of
Ibrahim's devotion.

Eid cards

On the occasion of both *Eids* it is customary to
congratulate a Muslim and/or send cards to arrive a day
or two in advance if you know him well. You may often
receive a card of thanks.

HOLY DAYS

Dates

The dates of the holy days shown below are subject
to change as the precise timing of some of them is
dependent on the sighting of the moon. Expatriates
will notice that, on many occasions, the announcement
of the dates involved may not occur until a day or
so beforehand.

---

29 In the two other monotheistic traditions it is Isaac who was about to be
sacrificed.

Lailat al-Qadr

The 'Night of Power' or 'Night of Determination' falls on one of the odd numbered nights during the last ten days of Ramadan (usually the night of the 27th); it commemorates the night on which the first divine revelations of the Koran were given to Mohammad (PBUH). Observance entails nightlong devotion and recitations.

Lailat al-Miraj

The 'Night Journey to Heaven', which falls on 27 *Rajab*, commemorates the vision of Mohammad's (PBUH) journey to Jerusalem and then to Heaven in which he was received by God.

Mawlid al-Nabi

The 'Prophet's Birthday' falls on 12 *Rabi' al-Awwal*, but its observance is traditional rather than Islamic, as Islam does not centre on any human being. Meetings are held, speeches made and prayers offered. (Note: not celebrated in Saudi Arabia.)

Ras as-Sana (New Year)

The 'Head of the Year' falls on 1 *Muharram*; it marks the time of Mohammad's migration (*Hejira*) from Makkah to Medina which is the beginning of the Islamic (or *Hejira*) calendar. *Ras as-Sana* can also refer to 1 January, when it is in order to send out Gregorian calendars, diaries and greetings cards to business colleagues. They should not contain any reference to Christmas. The standard greeting is "*Kull 'aam wa antum bikhair*".

Ashura

Ashura, which falls on 10 *Muharram*, is the *Shiite* commemoration of the death of Mohammad's (PBUH) grandson, Husayn, at the Battle of Kerbela in AD 680.

MUSLIM RULES ON DIET

Halal and *Haram*

The Koran lays down rules on which foods are permitted (*halal*) and which are forbidden (*haram*). There are numerous quotations in the Koran about eating habits. The following may not be consumed by a Muslim:

- Animals which have died a natural death or been killed for reasons other than food. This includes sacrifices to pagan deities, or animals not slaughtered in the prescribed manner. Animals killed for food (with the exception of seafood) have to be slaughtered in a certain way by a Muslim.
- Blood.
- Pork and its bi-products such as lard and gelatines.
- Alcohol and all fermented liquids including liquids or solid food containing alcoholic extracts (e.g. sherry trifle). It is most unwise to become involved in any activity (such as home-brewing) which has any connection whatsoever with the availability, distribution or sale of alcohol to Muslims.

Appendix – Arab Groupings

The League of Arab States (The Arab League)

Algeria	Lebanon	Saudi Arabia
Bahrain	Libya	Somalia
Comoros	Mauritania	Sudan
Djibouti	Morocco	Syria
Egypt	Oman	Tunisia
Iraq	Palestine	UAE
Jordan	Qatar	Yemen
Kuwait		

The League of Arab States (more often called the Arab League) is the oldest pan-Arab organisation, founded in 1945. Its aim is to co-ordinate policies and activities towards the common good of all Arab states.

From its formation, the Arab League has played an important political role in promoting independence from colonial rule. All members of the League must be independent Arab states. Palestine is considered an independent state and therefore a full member of the League. Every member country is represented on the Council, the supreme body of the Arab League, which meets twice a year, being presided over by each member state in turn. Additional, extraordinary sessions are held if requested by at least two member states.

The Secretary-General heads the Secretariat and is appointed by the Council for a five-year term of office.

In 1990 the permanent headquarters of the Arab League was re-established in Cairo after operating from Tunis for eleven years.

There are sixteen committees attached to the Council which handle political, cultural, economic, social, administrative, financial and legal affairs together with matters such as health, human rights, communications, oil, meteorology, and youth welfare. Many specialised organisations have emanated from the League of Arab States and these now form an integral part of the League, providing a framework for co-operation between Arab states and the rest of the world. For example, the Organisation of Arab Petroleum Exporting Countries (OAPEC) although not an Arab League agency, works closely with it. The League organisations have initiated research, development and training programmes. Joint chambers of commerce have been set up to encourage greater integration between Arab states and the world's leading trading and industrial nations.

Arab League offices and information centres have been set up in a number of countries throughout the world. The League maintains a permanent office at the United Nations and has observer status at the UN General Assembly.

The Arab Monetary Fund, established in 1977, does not focus on a particular commodity but aims to assist member states financially, functioning both as a fund and as a bank. More recently established bodies are the Arab *Maghreb* Union and the Arab Co-operation Council created in February 1989.

The Gulf Co-operation Council (GCC)
(See the map on page 5)

Bahrain	Qatar
Kuwait	Saudi Arabia
Oman	UAE

Formation

On February 4, 1981, the Foreign Ministers of the United Arab Emirates, Bahrain, Saudi Arabia, Oman, Qatar and Kuwait, met in Riyadh to co-ordinate and develop co-operation between these states. As a result of this meeting, a complete text of the organisational structure of the Gulf Co-operation Council (GCC) was issued:

'Due to the special links which exist between the United Arab Emirates, Bahrain, Saudi Arabia, Oman, Qatar and Kuwait, which arise from their common ideology, their similar statutes, the unity of their heritage, the similarities of their political, social and demographic structures, and the closeness of their culture; and since these states desire to deepen, develop and strengthen co-operation and co-ordination between them in various fields for the benefit, development and stability of their peoples, the Foreign Ministers of these countries met in Riyadh on February 4, 1981, for a consultation in order to set up an organisational and political structure to crystallise and develop the desired co-operation and co-ordination between these states. They agreed to form a council for co-operation between the above-mentioned Arab Gulf states, to establish a Secretariat-General for this purpose and to convene regular meetings at summit level, and at foreign minister level, to achieve the desired aims of these states and their peoples in all fields.

These steps are in accordance with the national aims of the Arab Nation within the constitution of the Arab League which encourages regional co-operation in order to strengthen the Arab Nation. They confirm the adherence of these states to the Arab League and the strengthening of their role in achieving the aims and principles of its constitution in order to serve the Arab and Islamic cause'.

On May 8, 1981, the Foreign Ministers of the six states held a meeting in Muscat, as a result of which the following text concerning the organisational statutes of the Co-operation Council was issued:

'Since the United Arab Emirates, Bahrain, Saudi Arabia, Oman, Qatar and Kuwait are aware of the special links between them, their common characteristics, similar systems and the importance of firm co-ordination between them in various fields, especially social and economic; and believing in their common aim and destiny, and their desire to achieve co-ordination and unity between them in all fields, these states decided to set up an organisation aiming to deepen and strengthen the links, relations and co-operation between the members. This organisation is called the Co-operation Council for the Arab States of the Gulf whose headquarters are in Riyadh in the Kingdom of Saudi Arabia. This Council is the means to achieving the maximum co-ordination and unity in all fields and for strengthening links and relations between its members in various fields. It is also the means for establishing similar systems in the fields of economics, finance, education, culture, health and social welfare, communications, information, passports and nationalities, travel and transportation, customs and trade affairs, the carriage of goods, and legal and legislative affairs'.

The Organisational Structure of the Co-operation Council

The Co-operation Council is composed of:
- The Supreme Council
- The Ministerial Council
- The Secretariat-General

Organisation of the Islamic Conference (OIC)
(See the map on page 106)

The Organisation of the Islamic Conference (OIC) was established in 1971 and has a permanent secretariat based in Jeddah, Saudi Arabia. The member states agree to 'consult together with one another with a view to promoting close co-operation and mutual assistance in the economic, scientific, cultural and spiritual fields, inspired by the immortal teachings of Islam.' Summit conferences are held every three years in a chosen member's country while Ministers of Foreign Affairs meet annually. The Organisation pledges humanitarian aid to Muslim communities affected by war, or natural disasters. Further detail is in Chapter 18 (see page 105).

Organisation of the Petroleum Exporting Countries (OPEC)

Algeria	Libya
Ecuador	Nigeria
Gabon	Qatar
Indonesia	Saudi Arabia
Iran	UAE
Iraq	Venezuela
Kuwait	

It is estimated that OPEC members possess 77 per cent of the world's known petroleum reserves, of which 66 per cent is in the Middle East, hence its inclusion in this Appendix, even though it is not an Arab grouping. Established in 1960, the Organisation of the Petroleum Exporting Countries

(OPEC) consists of the countries shown above. The Organisation was formed to link countries whose main source of export is petroleum and aims to unify and co-ordinate policies and safeguard members' interests.

The conference meets at least twice a year, once in Vienna and once in the capital of a member country, to decide on reports and recommendations submitted by a board of Governors. It works on the unanimity principle.

Organisation of Arab Petroleum Exporting Countries (OAPEC)

Algeria	Libya
Bahrain	Qatar
Egypt	Saudi Arabia
Iraq	Syria
Kuwait	UAE

The Organisation of Arab Petroleum Exporting Countries (OAPEC) was established in 1968 to safeguard the interests of members and to determine ways and means for their co-operation in the petroleum industry. The Council meets twice yearly. Topics covered include technical matters, legal aspects and economic studies. Activities were severely disrupted by the invasion of Kuwait by Iraq in 1990 and a temporary headquarters was set up in Cairo. The headquarters in Kuwait has now been reinstated.

Bibliography and publications

Books and publications

MAULVI ABDUL AZIZ, *Studies in Islam*, The Indian Islahia Centre,
Dubai, 1996

MOHAMMAD AL-FAHIM, *From Rags to Riches*,
The London Centre for Arab Studies, 1995

ABDUL RAHMAN BIN HAMMAD AL-OMAR, *The Religion of Truth*,
Ministry of Islamic Affairs, Riyadh, 1412 AH

MICHAEL ASHER, *Thesiger*, Motivate, 1994

HAMID ATIYYAH, *How to Live and Work in the Gulf*, How To Books, 1995

Bradman's Business Guide (Middle East), Monomax, 1998

MICHAEL FIELD, *Inside the Arab World*, John Murray, 1994

SIR DONALD HAWLEY, *Manners and Correct Form in the Middle East*,
Debrett's, 1984, Michael Russell, 1996

FRAUKE HEARD-BEY, *From Trucial States to United Arab Emirates*,
Longman, 1997

EDWARD HENDERSON, *This Strange Eventful History*, Quartet, 1988

PATRICIA HOLDEN, *Mother without a Mask*, Kyle Cathie, 1991,
Motivate, 1991

T.E. LAWRENCE, *Seven Pillars of Wisdom*, Doubleday, 1926

BERNARD LEWIS, *The Arabs in History*, Hutchinson, 1958 – 66,
Harper Torchbook, 1960 – 67

MEED Gulf Practical Guides, EMAP Business International, 1990 – 98

MARGARET NYDELL, *Understanding Arabs*, Intercultural Press, 1987

JAMES PETERS, *The Arab World Handbook*, Longman, 1989

SIR WILFRED THESIGER, *Arabian Sands*, Longman, 1959,
Motivate, 1994

FONS TROMPENAARS, *Riding the Waves of Culture*, Nicholas Brealey, 1993

Web sites

Islamic programmes
http://www.uwm.edu/cgi-bin/bashir/salat.cgi
http://www.solat.net

The Organisation of the Islamic Conference
http://www.sesrtcic.org

Meanings of Islamic expressions
http://www.usc.edu/dept/MSA/reference/glossary.html

The Author
e-mail: jjw@handshaikh.com
website: http://www.handshaikh.com

Index